Professional Learning Communities:

An Implementation Guide and Toolkit

Kathleen A. Foord & Jean M. Haar

EYE ON EDUCATION

6 DEPOT WAY WEST, SUITE 106

LARCHMONT, NY 10538

(914) 833–0551

(914) 833–0761 fax

www.eyeoneducation.com

Library of Congress Cataloging-in-Publication Data

Foord, Kathleen A.
Professional learning communities : an implementation guide and toolkit / Kathleen A. Foord and Jean M. Haar.
     p. cm.
   Includes bibliographical references and index.
ISBN 978-1-59667-088-4
1. Adult learning. 2. Educational leadership. 3. School improvement programs. 4. Educational change. I. Haar, Jean M. II. Title.
LC5225.L42F66 2008
374—dc22

                                     2008017414

10 9 8 7 6 5 4 3 2 1

Also Available from EYE ON EDUCATION

Meet the Authors

Kathleen (Kitty) Foord is the Coordinator of Professional Development and Department Chair at Minnesota State University in Mankato, Minnesota. She was a teacher, curriculum and assessment coordinator, and professional development specialist in public schools for 28 years before moving to higher education. During that time, she used learning communities to enhance teacher commitment to student achievement. In her current role, she teaches graduate courses related to improving teaching, assessment, leadership, and learning communities. She consults with school districts to provide professional development on coaching and learning communities.

Jean Haar is the Director for the Center for Engaged Leadership and Associate Professor at Minnesota State University in Mankato, Minnesota. She was a teacher and principal in public schools for 17 years before moving to higher education. Her experiences led her to understand and value the role of leadership in promoting professional growth to increase student learning. In addition to teaching courses in educational administration, she consults with school districts to provide professional development on leadership and learning communities.

Acknowledgments

There is a saying that "when the student is ready, the teacher will come." We have been blessed with so many teachers in our journey to understand professional learning communities. It is with deep appreciation that we first acknowledge the hundreds of educators and leaders whose ideas, practices, and questions have shaped our thinking. Your challenges became our challenges, your courage became our courage, and your convictions became our convictions. Each of us has also participated in professional learning communities and we wish to thank our colleagues in those communities. It is with you that we experienced community and learned to "walk the talk."

We wish to thank our College of Education colleagues who work with us to build a positive professional learning community. We especially wish to thank College of Education Dean, Michael Miller, whose belief in our work and philosophy has enabled us to immerse ourselves in our commitment to serve K-12 schools.

We wish to express our deep appreciation to our graduate advisors, Vivian Johnson and Marilyn Grady, whose encouragement and guidance nurtured our thinking, research, and writing.

We are grateful that we are working on our first book with Bob Sickles, publisher at Eye on Education. He has coached us with patience, enthusiasm, and respectful questions throughout the process.

Most importantly, we wish to acknowledge our families. Kitty is grateful for Karl, Andrew, Adam, and Jessica while Jean is grateful for Joel, Robert, and Megan. They know that we are driven by our passion to improve teaching, learning, and leading and provide unconditional support and encouragement to follow those passions. We thank them for this important gift.

Table of Contents

Free Downloads

A common purpose of a Professional Learning Community is to develop the means to address change. This book features eight **Innovation Maps** to help leaders and teachers assess and sustain PLCs.

Buyers of this book have permission to download and print out these **Innovation Maps** as Adobe Acrobat documents.

You can access these downloads by visiting Eye On Education's website:

www.eyeoneducation.com. Click on FREE Downloads or search or browse our website from our homepage to find this book and then scroll down for downloading instructions.

You'll need your book-buyer access code: **PLC-7088-4**

1

Effective Professional Learning Communities

The current popularity of professional learning communities (PLCs) raises many questions for leaders as they develop a vision for PLCs in their schools. Why should we use PLCs? What are the most important elements, components, or functions in a PLC? How do we get them started and keep them going? How do we know when PLCs are working well or on the verge of failure? What is the role of the teacher and the leader in developing and sustaining PLCs? These and other questions flood the thoughts of leaders across the nation as they read, study, and implement PLCs. Each of the leaders works in a different setting, with different students, teachers, parents, and politics. Are the answers to these questions the same in each setting or dependent on the context?

In this book, we guide you in developing your capacity to lead PLCs as you answer the hard questions with the right answer for your personal context. Leadership comes in many forms and is most effective when shared to create collective responsibility for change. This book can support the PLC leadership capacity of everyone in a school or district.

- ◆ Teachers can use this book to increase student achievement, shape their own professional growth, work effectively with colleagues, become more accountable for results, and develop interdependence with other educators and leaders within their school and district.

- ◆ Teacher leaders can use this book to develop shared leadership and responsibility for increased student achievement, focused professional growth, effective interpersonal relationships in PLCs, increased accountability and increased interdependence among educators and leaders in their school and district.

- ◆ Principals can use this book to strengthen instructional leadership that supports increased student achievement, coaching for professional growth, development of effective structural and relational change in policies and practices, and assured accountability, interdependence, and sustainability for effective PLCs in their school and district.

1

♦ Superintendents and other district office leaders can use this book to align and support policies, practices, and resources needed by schools to develop effective PLCs that increase student and professional growth and that assure accountability, interdependence, and sustainability for effective PLCs among schools within the district.

We begin by introducing you to a leader, who much like you, seeks to increase her capacity to lead through the use of effective PLCs.

Vignette 1

Teresa had been a principal for seven years following eight years as a classroom teacher. She really wanted her staff to be less dependent on her to solve school problems and more professionally committed to addressing student needs. She wanted more distributed responsibility for decisions in her building.

Principals in her district had completed a book study on professional learning communities (PLCs) and agreed to try some practices. She shared her vision for PLCs at a faculty meeting in January. During faculty meetings, teachers read articles on PLCs and developed a list of elements needed in PLCs. At the end of the year, Teresa asked a group of teachers to serve as the PLC leadership team. They looked at their school's list of PLC elements and student achievement data to develop a vision, a mission, and goals for the next year.

She knew there were skeptical teachers who were likely to resist PLCs during the next year and wondered what physical, academic, and social structures would increase the likelihood of successful PLC implementation.

Guiding Questions

♦ Why should we use PLCs?

♦ Why do we need to develop structural and relational practices for successful implementation of PLCs?

♦ How can we analyze our assumptions and information about PLCs for effective implementation?

Let's start by developing an understanding about why we recommend the use of PLCs. There is considerable evidence about how PLCs increase teacher and student achievement, and we will explore that in a moment. However, most teachers and leaders want to know that something works in the real world, not just in a research study. So, we decided to start by sharing a few of our own stories that have led to our study and commitment to PLCs. We think it is important to walk the talk and that our credibility and confidence come from the ability to reflect on our personal experiences. We each share stories about what has and has not worked in our journey to use PLCs.

Kitty's Story

I worked as a curriculum and assessment specialist in two school districts as the standards movement came into full swing. There were state-level initiatives to teacher-proof the delivery of standards through implementation of core assessments. Even if the state assessments didn't fit the context, teaching skills, or style, or even the district adopted materials; teachers were encouraged to work as a team to implement the state assessments. I worked with teams of teachers to understand how the new standards matched their own outcomes and materials and helped them develop their own core assessments. I experienced all the elements of resistance that come with major teacher-change initiatives. "This will pass; this is inappropriate for my discipline; what will you do if I don't comply; this is a waste of precious teaching time; this is causing interdepartmental conflict, you can't make me work with that teacher; our community will rally around us to stop this; this is not really part of my job description; how much are you going to pay me to do it; there's no time to do this," and so on. I learned a great deal during that time about what doesn't work and what does work when implementing teacher change. Treating teachers as delivery technicians instead of professionals didn't afford them the respect or recognition they deserved as well-educated adults and ensured dependent or resistant behavior would continue.

I earned my master's and doctoral degrees in settings that were effective PLCs. Those experiences supported significant change in my own practices and beliefs and in those of my colleagues. This led to extensive personal research into learning communities, adult learning, change, and professional practices. Seven state-sponsored grants permitted me to use this research to study PLCs. One of the grants became the focus of my dissertation on how professional development in learning communities influences changes in teacher beliefs and practices. This work revealed that professional expertise increased significantly as did the ability to reflect, to self-direct learning, to learn with others, and to assume leadership responsibility for the learning of others. I am a product of and now a committed facilitator in several districts for effective PLCs because I know that they can increase teacher professionalism, and, therefore, student achievement.

Jean's Story

I began my professional career in a small, rural school district. The level of personal attention I could provide students and, in turn, their open, honest communication about what they were or were not learning served as valuable learning experiences for me not only about student learning but also about effective teaching. I also realized that a number of factors that occurred outside my classroom greatly impacted my students' ability to learn within my classroom. It did not take me long to realize the important role leadership played in creating an atmosphere conducive to teaching and learning. The foundation I gained from my teaching experience prepared me for the challenges I faced as a building principal who was intent on creating a culture focused on respect and high expectations for student and adult learning.

As a principal, I had staff members who were committed to their profession and who cared about students. What I did not have was a structure or a culture that promoted professional learning as a community. Teachers were pursuing their own professional growth based on what was brought to their attention and what was available. Often times the opportunities focused on content or technology—little focused on student learning.

During my years as a principal, I consistently faced issues where teachers' efforts to create powerful learning experiences for their students were meet with obstacles. These obstacles included (a) expecting teachers to envision and plan for all learning experiences a year in advance (without allowing teachers to become familiar with student needs and then determine appropriate learning experiences); (b) expecting teachers to develop, implement, and score comprehensive exams that promote critical thinking in conjunction with expecting them to submit the final grades in a short time frame; (c) being asked to appropriately incorporate technology into the curriculum with basic technology application training; and (d) being asked to complete budget requests, to determine facility needs, and to determine supplies for next year in the midst of teaching. These as well as other policies and procedures hindered our abilities to be innovative, to explore new strategies, and to take the risks needed to improve student learning. Most of the policies and procedures were created for efficiency rather than effectiveness—many were also developed before the existing era of educational accountability and change.

During my principalship and through my doctoral studies, I continually investigated ways in which school leaders were effectively creating environments conducive to student and teacher growth. The research on PLCs provided me with an understandable concept and a framework. PLCs are an opportunity for schools to replace dated policies and procedures and to develop a culture that promotes high expectations for all while respecting student and adult learning. PLCs also serve as a framework for building a sense of community within a district—something I believe is desperately needed as schools continue to face the enormous challenges that accompany the needs of an ever-changing, global society.

Why Should We Use Professional Learning Communities?

There is growing evidence that documents improved teaching and learning with the use of PLCs. Recent work (DuFour & Eaker, 1998) offers strong testimony of the significant changes in student achievement that can occur in single schools. What does the wider body of research across various schools reveal? Work by Newman, Wehlage, & Secada (1996) indicates significant student gains regardless of school demographics when teachers worked collaboratively to apply, assess, and analyze authentic standards and assessments. Hall and Hord (2001) document increases in teacher learning and implementation of teacher learning communities for improved student results. They also indicate that improved collaboration among teachers and administrators is an essential factor in effective teacher community. McLaughlin and Talbert (2006) also report improved teaching and learning from a synthesis of recent studies:

A wide range of statistical data supports the claim that school-based PLCs improve teaching and learning. Evidence includes:

a. Positive effects of teacher learning community measures on student achievement for both regional and nationally representative school samples;

b. Strong correlations of teacher learning community with teaching practices that predict student learning gains; and

c. Strong correlations of teacher learning community and student experiences of the school and class. (p. 9)

Using data from the National Longitudinal Study of 1988 (Scott & Ingels, 2007) researchers found that students do better academically in a school with collaborative teacher communities and that in these schools socioeconomic status had less effect on their achievement gains (Lee & Smith, 1995, 1996; Lee, Smith, & Coninger, 1997 as quoted in McLaughlin & Talbert, 2006, p. 9).

The use of learning communities by math and science teachers resulted in changes in practice that involved increased communication density, intensified instructional practice norms, and increased consistency in practice (Yasumoto, Uekawa, & Bidwell, 2001): "The study provides statistical evidence to argue that teacher learning communities develop knowledge of practice that is beyond the sum of competent and innovative teachers" (p. 10). Deep, social construction about the meaning and application of teaching practice by groups of teachers can lead to an exponential impact through teacher synergy and consistency of practice.

Research is revealing a correlation between collegial relationships among teachers and how students respond with respect, participation, and academic self-efficacy in the classroom (Center for Research on Context of Teaching, 2002 as cited in McLaughlin & Talbert, 2006, p. 10). The evidence clearly beckons us to implement PLCs to improve teaching and learning. The evidence is less clear about the PLC structural and relational practices that create effective, collaborative PLCs.

Much of the recent literature has focused on listing elements needed for the structural design of PLCs. Schlechty (1997, p. 136), however, reminds us that "structural change that is not supported by cultural change will eventually be overwhelmed by the culture, for it is in the culture that any organization finds education reform." We agree and in subsequent chapters will outline the structural and relational changes in practices that can lead to effective PLCs.

Why Do We Need to Develop Structural and Relational Practices at the Same Time for Professional Learning Community Success?

Hundreds of schools and districts have implemented structural practices to use PLCs over the last several years. They put in place well-articulated missions, visions, values, and goals. They arranged teachers into PLC groups, set regular meeting times, used meeting protocols, and developed PLC reporting systems. As they moved into defining essential outcomes, core assessments, and consistent teaching practices, they started to experience teacher push-back.

Often after the first year or two of structural practices, pleas for strategies to make teachers work effectively together come from administrators and pleas to get rid of PLCs come from teachers. Administrators and teacher leaders have valiantly tried to implement the physical structures of PLCs but have met with limited success because effective relational and change practices are absent. They have discovered that coming together does not lead to effectively working together much less to staying together.

The leading proponents of PLCs (DuFour & Eaker 1998; DuFour et al., 2004, 2005, 2006) argue that commitment to PLCs will dramatically change practices and produce results for student achievement. Do changes in beliefs (commitment) lead to changes in practice or do changes in practice lead to changes in beliefs? How you answer that question is important. Considerable new research suggests that changes in practice lead to changes in beliefs (Blankstein, 2004; Foord, 2004; Fullan, 2002; Hord, 2004).

DuFour et al. (2004) also state that "a school that focuses exclusively on responding to students who are having difficulty without also developing the capacity of every administrator and teacher to become more effective will fail to become a professional learning community" (p. 37). We heartily agree and believe that developing effective structural and relational practices leads to a belief in and commitment to PLCs. A "tight" administrative expectation for student achievement with a "loose" hand on methods to achieve those results does not address the ever present resistance to change in an educational system characterized by privatized practices. Developing effective practices for change by administrators and teachers means we must focus on teacher and leader learning, organizational learning, relational learning, interdependent groups and systems, decision-making processes, and individual and group accountability.

We suggest that a tight expectation on development of teacher, leader, and organizational capacity in these areas will permit a loose hand on the methods to achieve remarkable student achievement. A key premise of DuFour et al. (2004) is that commitment to PLCs by teachers will produce results. With commitment (a belief) we will do

> Commitment is the result that comes from continuously sharing understanding and creating meaning, engaging in new learning with practice and application, reflecting on practices with feedback, and collaborating with others to improve over time.

"whatever it takes" (our practice). We think that the reverse is true. Commitment is the result that comes from continuously sharing understanding and creating meaning, engaging in new learning with practice and application, reflecting on practices with feedback, and collaborating with others to improve over time. The continuous improvement cycle must be applied not only to improve student learning but to improve learning for teachers, administrators, schools, and districts. The "tight" control should not be on commitment to a mission and student achievement results but to a process that permits professionals to learn with one another so that they are able to address the changing needs of all learners in the educational system.

DuFour et al. (2004) state, "It is imperative that staff members demonstrate a willingness to change some traditional assumptions, practices, roles, and responsibilities" (p. 37). If a willingness to change is imperative for PLCs to succeed, how does an administrator develop this willingness to change? Willing yourself into a change is like willing yourself to lose weight or to quit smoking. The commitment will be short-lived if it lacks ongoing support for small changes in practices that eventually lead to full commitment to the change. The existing PLC literature is largely silent on how to facilitate the small, ongoing changes in practices that lead to commitment to PLCs. In this book, we outline a comprehensive process and specific practices to support the incremental changes that are needed to successfully navigate your way to committed, effective PLCs.

Why do we need to go beyond structural practices to focus on relational practices? We suggest four key reasons for moving beyond structural practices in the development of PLCs.

1. *We want professionals not technicians.* We are not content with teachers who deliver lessons from the text during their eight-hour duty shift. We are not content with teachers who merely attend required parent teacher conferences to report on the progress of their students without a plan to enlist parental cooperation. A technically proficient teacher lacks the energy, creativity, and determination to reach each child. We want teachers who plan and implement rich, developmentally appropriate curriculum in ways that are instructionally responsive to the diverse students in their classrooms. We want teachers who connect to other professionals, to parents, and to the community in ways that promote healthy, collaborative relationships that support student learning. We want teachers who are passionate about their profession and who clearly demonstrate that they care about their students.

2. *We want our teachers to act and learn as adults not as children.* We are not content with requiring professional development workshops for all teachers that punctuate the school calendar three times a year. We see little engagement in new learning by our teachers and even less direct impact on changes in practice or student learning. We are disheartened by the number of teachers who call in sick on professional development days. We are tired of hearing complaints that teachers can't respond to the diverse students in their classrooms because there isn't enough time to learn new teaching strategies such as differentiation. We are frustrated with parceling out scarce professional development funds with no system to assure that they will increase teacher skill or impact student learning. We are tired of faculty meetings where teachers grade papers, carry on private conversations, fail to contribute to the large group discussions, or simply don't show up. We dream of individual professional growth plans tied to each teacher's needs to increase student achievement. We imagine teacher-managed growth plans that document professional development, practice, and reflection with other professionals on a daily basis. Just as we hope for differentiated instruction for our students we hope for differentiated learning for our teachers. We want job-embedded learning where adults enthusiastically self-direct their professional practices with each other in response to real student needs.

3. *We want positive interdependence with our teachers not dependence on us as the leader.* We are not content with teachers who wait for us to tell them our goals and direction for the year. We cannot

> We want teachers who are passionate about their profession and who clearly demonstrate that they care about their students.

micromanage each teacher or even each initiative in the building if we want to see progress in several areas. We are tired of having teachers ask us what we are going to do about the myriad problems from changing standards, curriculum, and assessments to changing demographics, parental involvement, and societal expectations. We want teachers who understand how issues affect us as a whole and initiate important work to serve our children, families, school and broader community. We cannot lead everything and need to develop leaders among our teachers whom we and others can follow.

4. *We want a successful, learning organization not just learning individuals.* We are not content with single teachers who develop high levels of professionalism. We are uncomfortable with the critical "catty" comments of teachers who try to place a ceiling on teachers who strive and therefore raise expectations for performance. We are disappointed when excellent teachers are unable to share their learning for the benefit of all and even more disappointed when they leave the profession for another career. We are jealous of schools that have high-functioning teams whose collaborative learning results in incredible student achievement increases. We are frustrated with how difficult it is to ensure that all schools reach such a high level of functional effectiveness. We want and need teachers who learn and grow together to produce synergistic, collective knowledge and responsibility to address student learning and organizational learning problems. We want to sustain the system so the organization remembers and responds, not just individual teachers. If one person leaves, the school success will continue.

How Can We Analyze Our Assumptions and Information about Professional Learning Communities for Effective Implementation?

In the current context of high accountability and sanctions from No Child Left Behind legislation, the lure of results from commitment to whatever it takes is incredibly attractive. We think that the opposite is more likely true, that success produces commitment. We worry that jumping from one district- or school-selected goal, strategy, or textbook to the next in search of success without the relational skills to achieve those goals in a PLC will ultimately lead to despair. When teachers seek to change their practices and are able to reflect on the causes of their success, they develop deep commitment to the practices that will continue to assure success. Going through motions spelled out by others without personal commitment and reflection is mere compliance. Professional learning communities can be an effective means to promote teacher change for student learning when the PLC focuses on personal commitment to changes in practices that lead to reflection on changes in their beliefs. Therefore, we need to understand what promotes changes in practices to use PLCs effectively. In this chapter we invite you to briefly examine existing assumptions that are applied to PLCs and some alternative assumptions that should be explored to unveil improvements in how we lead in PLCs. In the next chapter, we explain in detail the important principles and theories about adult learning, teacher change, and relational capacity that govern our suggestions for changes in how we develop and lead PLCs.

The current design and use of PLCs rests on assumptions about how teachers change, learn, and interact that deserve careful rethinking. Senge, Cambron-McCabe, Lucas, Smith, Dutton, & Kleiner in *Schools That Learn* (2000) advised learning organizations to carefully examine assumptions, values, and beliefs behind actions to assure commitment to change. We invite you to examine the assumptions of previous authors, the assumptions of your organization, the assumptions of your teachers, the assumptions that you hold, and the assumptions that we share as you develop your understanding of your role as a leader for effective PLCs. As you review these assumptions, we encourage you to continually ask the question "Why?" We find that asking the question why, several times in a row, helps us to surface our assumptions and develop our understanding and commitment to practice. Much like the two-year-old who needs to know "why" before committing to the new practices suggested by a parent, we need to know why we are committing to PLC practices so that we understand and can answer teachers who will ask "why" in many oppositional ways as we implement PLCs.

Assumptions and Insights about Teacher Change

Three assumptions about change govern much of the current literature and many existing PLC initiatives. First, we assume that leaders can direct or persuade staff to make a commitment to change with tightly constructed missions, visions, values, goals, or outcomes. Second, we assume that public reporting and exploration of data about unmet standards or benchmarks can convince or shame teachers into a commitment to change. Finally, we assume that individual teachers in PLCs can effectively design changes in practice to meet tightly constructed outcomes with little intervention or support. None of these current assumptions is supported by the research on change.

There are five principles of change that have implications for the design and implementation of effective PLCs.

1. There is a growing body of research to indicate that changes in practices lead to changes in beliefs (Caine & Caine, 1997b; Evans, 1996; Foord, 2004; Fullan, 1995, Guskey, 2000: Hall & Hord, 2001; Toole, 2001) and not the other way around. Attempting to persuade teachers to align their practices to district beliefs such as mission, vision, or goals will not promote changes in practice if those beliefs are not already held by the teachers.

2. Change comes when teachers share a common concern and commit to changes because of a common purpose. However, Hall and Hord (2001) outline multiple levels of concern and use through which teachers must

proceed as they adopt innovations. Common purpose is not one imposed from without but one that is developed through deep discussion and reflection on commonly held values over a period of time as the innovation is used. Purposes and values will vary from PLC to PLC, so a tightly held school or district value may or may not be embraced by individual teachers in a PLC without experiencing a change in practice over time that leads to that value.

3. Change in practice requires clear targets for effective professional practices and specific, frequent feedback on proficiency (Danielson, 1996; NBPTS, 1989; Stiggins, Arter, Chappuis, & Chappuis, 2006).

4. Changes in practice are the result of time spent in a cycle of implementation that honors four stages of change: understanding, personalization, operationalization, and evaluation (Hall & Hord, 2001; Foord, 2004).

5. Effective change can be enhanced by monitoring the level of use of new practices and supporting higher levels of implementation (Hall & Hord, 2001).

Assumptions and Insights about Adult Learning

Despite extensive research about best practices for professional development, schools continue to plan professional development days or events assuming that if they provide the learning opportunity, learning will occur and practices will change. Typically, the topics for this learning are selected by a committee. Sometimes the selection is based on student needs and sometimes it is based on which "expert" is available for hire on that day. When schools use data, standards, or goals as the foci of their professional development, there is an assumption that this focus will lead teachers to a clear understanding of changes needed in their teaching practices. There is also an assumption that adults learn similarly to one another and can be trained in uniform ways to produce uniform learning. In PLCs this can look like a required, common agenda to be discussed in all groups on a specific day. This belief is held in spite of increasing evidence of the importance of differentiation for students. It is difficult to change a belief about differentiation without experiencing the practice first. Finally, there is an assumption that if adults learn a new teaching strategy, the learning will translate into a change in practice. Without systematic, effective use of the strategy followed by reflection on its impact and importance to student learning, the learning will disappear within a week.

There are several adult learning principles that impact PLC success. First, adults prefer to measure their learning against professional standards (Danielson, 1996; Foord, 2004). They need to see the relevance of their learn-

Adults, just like children, need clear and stable targets to motivate learning and develop their sense of self and collective efficacy.

ing to the improvement in their own practice. Adults, just like children, need clear and stable targets to motivate learning and develop their sense of self and collective efficacy (Stiggins et al., 2006). Second, adults prefer to construct their learning in social settings with reflection on the impact of their learning to solve real problems or concerns that they have chosen. Adults learn best when their efforts are self-directed and when they negotiate the meaning of their learning through social transactions (Merriam, Cafferella, & Baumgartner, 2007). Research on adult learning also indicates that a cycle of learning that develops understanding for the need for change, allows personalization of commitment and learning, encourages practice with reflection on results, and promotes collaboration to improve practices results in significant changes in practice (Foord, 2004).

Assumptions and Insights about Adult Interaction

The simple act of grouping adults together does not result in an effective learning community. One of the primary reasons why PLCs fail is poor adult interactions in groups. All sorts of conflict behaviors raise their ugly heads. If adults learn best through social transaction, then attention to adult interactions, including interpersonal and group skills, is needed. Some assume that assigning leaders for each PLC will result in effective interactions. Unfortunately assigned leadership does not guarantee effective followership. Finally, it is assumed that strict meeting protocols and hierarchical reporting structures will improve PLC interactions. However, PLC groups learn to file the proper forms with little impact on interactions, teacher change, or student learning.

Professional learning communities need to support four conditions for effective adult interaction. First, relationships need to foster interdependence reflected in shared norms, goals, outcomes, assessments, and practices. Second, significant, effective interpersonal interaction, preferably face to face interaction, is needed to permit social construction of meaning. Third, understanding of various approaches to conflict and conflict management strategies are needed. Finally, interactions should promote both individual and group accountability and responsibility.

Assumptions and Insights about
Effective Professional Learning Community Meetings

If only there was a simple "how-to" book that schools could follow to guarantee effective PLC meetings. There is a common assumption that protocols, agendas, and forms will produce effective meetings. Another assumption is that a regularly scheduled time and consistent elements in each meeting will create a successful community. Some believe that success will naturally come if every meeting focuses complete attention on student learning.

In reality, there are four types of meetings that support the stages in the learning and change cycle. Informational meetings help teachers identify student and teacher learning needs. Learning meetings help teachers commit to new learning to improve their practice, their interactions, and support improved student learning. Application meetings permit teachers to discuss and analyze the practice of new skills. Finally, reflection, evaluation, and collaboration meetings help teachers assess the impact of new practices on student learning and teacher practices and to extend their individual practice through synergy with others. Topics, time, agendas, and protocols must change to match the various meeting needs. All meetings must address teacher learning and changes in practice needed to support student learning. If all meetings focus on students and getting student results, there is a tendency for teachers to look for the "flaw" and the "fix" in the student. Change is sought externally. If all meetings focus on teacher practices and developing collective teacher capacity to meet the needs of students, change and improvement is moved squarely to the shoulders of teachers. Change is sought internally by the teacher and in relationship with other teachers.

Assumptions and Insights about Student Learning

When the focus of PLCs is to do whatever it takes to increase student achievement, it is often assumed that more time and additional interventions will bring about results in student learning. If the student is not learning in class, add tutoring, then add mentoring, then add counseling. Unfortunately, this assumption reflects a common misconception that the deficiency for learning rests in the student, not in the curriculum, methods of instruction, or means of assessment. Teachers complain that they taught the lessons but the students just didn't learn them. When there are doubts about the ability of teachers to teach effectively it is often assumed that a more rigorous, research-based text or method should be adopted to provide uniform teaching and learning for students, making the learning teacher-proof. The underlying, flawed assumption is that all children learn in the same way and that more of the same content and instruction for longer periods will increase student motivation and learning.

Effective student learning is supported by ensuring that every teacher is an effective professional who actively seeks ways to improve their practice. Individual teachers working in PLCs must bear the responsibility for changing practices to meet the needs of each student in their charge. Data must be used by PLCs to address individual students' readiness, interest, and learning styles. Curriculum, instruction, and assessment must be differentiated in the regular classroom. Additional support systems and interventions should be available when demonstrated differentiation efforts have not met a student's needs. Learning must be rigorous, relevant, and supportive of healthy relationships among students, teachers, and the community at large. Motivation to learn must be supported through clear targets and specific frequent feedback.

Assumptions and Insights
about Vision-Driven Action Plans

An assumption of many PLC advocates is that a clear vision will drive effective action. However, vision statements often lack the clarity and direction to permit action. We want to take a moment to explore the big picture (vision) before launching into the detailed steps (action) you can take to create effective PLCs. Implementation is sometimes thwarted when the detailed steps are provided without the big picture. Likewise, the big picture without the detailed steps can limit the extent of implementation. We will briefly explore the big picture now in Chapter 1, move into the details of implementation in Chapter 2 through Chapter 7, and come back to the big picture in Chapter 8.

Professional learning community advocates recommend implementation of a pyramid of student interventions when educators discover that students are not achieving at expected levels. These can result in a Band-Aid approach to "fixing" individual students but fail to analyze and develop a systematic approach to increasing student achievement. Without a corresponding pyramid of interventions to change teaching practices, the Band-Aid interventions will likely need to be repeated again and again. Systematic use of increasingly specific data will also help us to understand which students need interventions and which teaching practices need improvement leading to less reliance on separate interventions when classroom learning fails. Figure 1.1 represents our image of a more systematic approach to change through three pyramids of intervention. In addition, the innovation maps and tools shared in this book will assist you in understanding and designing pyramids of intervention to address needs in your school or district. Once you have had the opportunity to analyze needs and assets through reading Chapters 2 through 7, this pyramid of interventions is revisited in Chapter 8.

Figure 1.1. Pyramid of Interventions

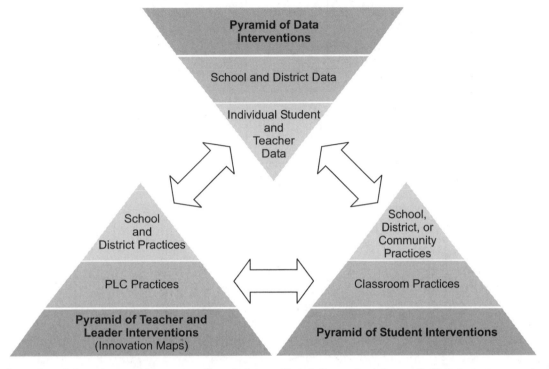

Another big picture process that is beneficial for schools and districts to use is the *change analysis framework.* We view PLCs as change forces that take us from our existing state to our desired state. The following change analysis framework (Figure 1.2) can guide educators and leaders in moving to the desired state using processes that are supported throughout the book with innovation maps, figures, and reflective questions.

The change analysis framework guides educators and leaders in moving from the existing state to the desired state of change.

Step 1.   In step one, we develop a deep understanding of our existing state by exploring the history, beliefs and values, assumptions, and policies and practices that currently shape the structures and cultures of our schools. Processes for surfacing these understandings are explored in Chapters 3 and 4.

Step 2.   In step two, we create a vision for our desired state by exploring principles and standards for effective adult learning, change, effective PLC development, and relational trust. Processes for developing this vision are explored in Chapters 2, 3, and 5.

Step 3.   In step three, we surface structural and cultural assets and barriers that minimize our movement to the desired state or vision. Processes for exploring these assets and barriers are explored in Chapters 4 through 7.

Figure 1.2. Change Analysis Framework

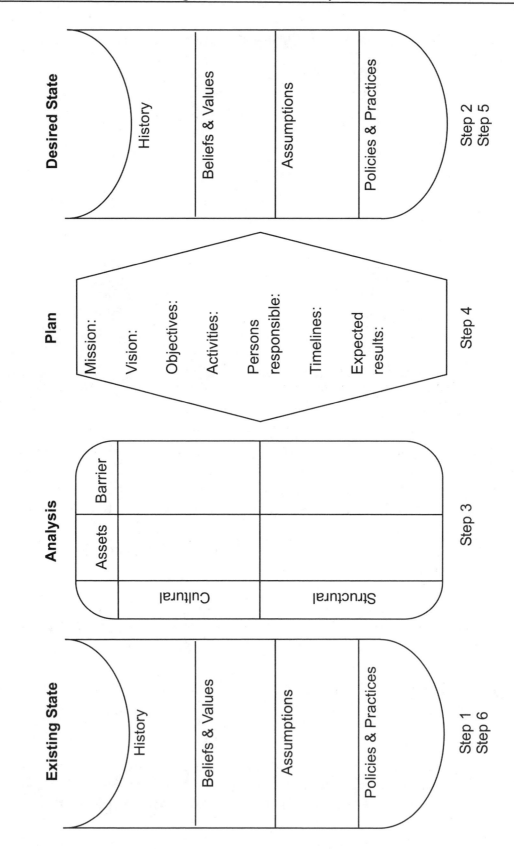

Step 4.   In step four, we develop action plans for change by removing barriers and enhancing assets to move to the desired state or vision. There are innovation maps, figures, reflective questions, and planning tools throughout Chapters 2 through 8 that will assist in this planning process.

Step 5.   In step five, we reflect on the implementation of our plans to determine the revised history we have created, our revised beliefs and values, our revised assumptions, and our revised policies and practices. Chapters 7 and 8 are especially valuable in outlining processes that permit deep reflection and analysis for sustainable changes.

Step 6.   In step six, we take the information in step five to refocus our change analysis for future improvements. This step starts the cycle all over again.

The symbols actually have meaning within the flow process that help us understand the role of each step within the change framework process (Figure 1.3).

Figure 1.3. Symbol Meaning in the Change Analysis Framework

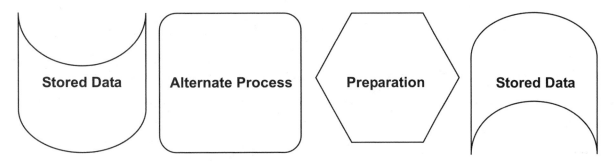

The following two figures demonstrate a completed change analysis framework using our discussion in Chapter 1. Figure 1.4 summarizes the existing state of our history, beliefs and values, assumptions, and policies and practices in typical PLCs as well as our desired state of PLCs that we hope will be achieved. Figure 1.5 summarizes the assets and barriers that are typical as well as the plan to use maps, tools, activities, and questions in this book to move PLCs to the desired state. It has been interesting for us to witness how a barrier in one school district may be an asset in another. For instance, we have observed one district struggle with the teacher contract in connection with PLC implementation whereas another district found the teacher contract served as an asset with PLC implementation; thus the reason for the same list assets/barriers and under structural/cultural but with different introductory phrases. We hope this summary will help you visualize the big picture of this change process before we move on to the specific change mechanisms that will permit us to complete the process.

Figure 1.4. Existing and Desired State Change Framework Examples

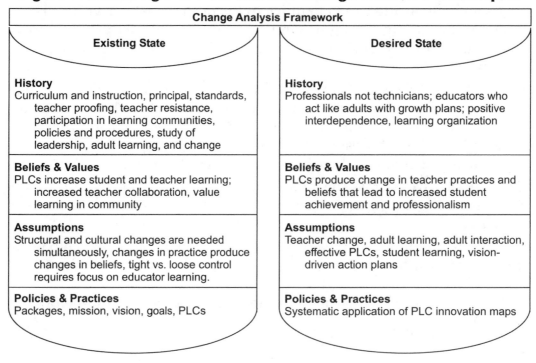

Change Analysis Framework	
Existing State	**Desired State**
History Curriculum and instruction, principal, standards, teacher proofing, teacher resistance, participation in learning communities, policies and procedures, study of leadership, adult learning, and change	**History** Professionals not technicians; educators who act like adults with growth plans; positive interdependence, learning organization
Beliefs & Values PLCs increase student and teacher learning; increased teacher collaboration, value learning in community	**Beliefs & Values** PLCs produce change in teacher practices and beliefs that lead to increased student achievement and professionalism
Assumptions Structural and cultural changes are needed simultaneously, changes in practice produce changes in beliefs, tight vs. loose control requires focus on educator learning.	**Assumptions** Teacher change, adult learning, adult interaction, effective PLCs, student learning, vision-driven action plans
Policies & Practices Packages, mission, vision, goals, PLCs	**Policies & Practices** Systematic application of PLC innovation maps

Figure 1.5. Analysis and Plan Change Framework Examples

Change Analysis Framework			
Analysis			**Plan**
	Assets	Barriers	**Mission:** Effective learning

		Assets	Barriers
Cultural		*Strength in...* Professionalism, Culturally responsive quality teaching, commitment, shared leadership, collaboration, collective responsibility	*Lack of...* Professionalism, culturally responsive quality teaching, commitment, shared leadership, collaboration, collective responsibility
Structural		*Support found in...* time, tests, NCLB, state standards, policies, procedures, unions, contracts, buildings, school calendars for professional development	*Constraints due to...* time, tests, NCLB, state standards, policies, procedures, unions, contracts, buildings, school calendars for professional development

Plan

Mission: Effective learning

Vision: Effective PLCs

Objectives:
1. Create effective PLC structures
2. Create effective PLC cultures
3. Promote learning and sustain change

Activities: Use innovation maps, activities, and reflection questions in this book

Persons responsible: You, other school leaders, leadership team, and teachers

Timelines: Determined by building and district

Expected results: Effective student growth and professional growth; sustainable PLCs

Change takes time and schools cannot expect to complete this change framework in one year. Indeed the framework is cyclical in nature and is repeated many times to execute the needed changes. In Chapter 8, we outline how this change analysis framework can be used to develop ongoing leadership action plans for progressive changes over time.

Looking Ahead

In Chapter 2, we explain in detail the important principles and theories about adult learning, teacher change, and relational practices that support a change cycle. We use the change cycle in the remaining chapters to model the change process for adult learners. Chapter 3 introduces a comprehensive system of innovation maps that will be used throughout the book to assess and sustain PLCs. The chapter focuses on student and teacher learning innovations. In Chapter 4, we guide you to explore the development of purpose, commitment, and structures for effective PLCs. Chapter 5 focuses on the development of relationally effective PLCs. We guide you to understand and construct meaning with others through interdependent collaboration using effective interpersonal skills, group processing, and accountability practices. In Chapter 6, you will learn how to use coaching to assess and encourage PLC development and success. Chapter 7 examines strategies for sustaining PLCs and change. Finally, in Chapter 8, we invite you to organize your reflections on current practices to develop a leadership plan for the implementation of effective, sustainable PLCs.

In each chapter, we will follow the story of Teresa (our composite leader) as she moves through the implementation of PLCs in her school. She will appear at the beginning of each chapter with concerns and at the end of the chapter with actions implemented in her journey through PLC development. Following the introductory vignette, we focus attention on several guiding questions about the development of one or more elements that are essential for effective PLCs. In each chapter these guiding questions are addressed using research and experiences in our work with PLCs. This "content" section is followed with specific suggestions or strategies to develop your capacity and competence in the PLC element(s). Each chapter allows you to self-assess your current understanding and level of implementation of the element(s) using detailed innovation maps. Your learning is extended when you assess the level of implementation achieved by Teresa in a post vignette. We also share with you our assessment of Teresa's level of implementation and make suggestions for new evidence and improvements needed to increase PLC success. Finally, reflective questions at the end of each chapter invite you to think about your own setting and the implications of this new learning on your leadership and PLC practices. We highly value reflective questions as the key to professional learning in community. We use questions throughout this text as a means to deepen learning. We don't always have answers but are entirely comfortable asking questions that will help us all become better seekers of meaning with our professional colleagues.

2

Look Before You Leap

Vignette 2

In June, Teresa's PLC leadership team developed the vision, mission, and goals for PLCs. How could they build a sense of ownership for the changes they planned? How would they create the energy and commitment for the work this would entail? How would they construct professional development that created changes in teacher practices? What were the best practices they could use to enhance adult learning, to increase commitment to new teaching practices, and to develop professional relationships? Teresa had some understanding of professional development and change strategies but feared that the work of building PLCs in her own complex setting required skills that she lacked. How would she engage her learners in building professional communities, constructing meaning, supporting learning, reflecting deeply, assessing expectations, and changing the culture? She had two months before her leadership team would meet again and she needed to learn more and hopefully gain greater confidence to lead.

Guiding Questions

- How do we create effective learning environments for adults?
- How do we influence change in teacher practices and beliefs?
- What conditions are needed for effective PLCs?
- How do we promote effective relationships in PLCs?

Some proponents of change suggest that we simply don't have time to study things in depth and that we should just take preliminary data and run with it. They aspire to the motto "Ready, Shoot, Aim." That may be appropriate when a budget crisis looms or when there are few choices available for a curriculum adoption. However, when it comes to implementing changes that rely on extensive human interactions for their success, as is the case in PLCs, it is better to understand the theories, principles, and practices that will support human change. Teachers are predictable in their rejection of policies and practices that don't respect adults, that call for rigid changes in practices with little buy-in, or that destroy relationships and build cultures of mistrust. If we implement under the guise of urgency, we may deal with resistance for years. If we attend to the human side of adult learning and change and we also take more careful aim, we can enlist support and build commitment for the long haul. This chapter will outline current theories, principles, and practices that will help us take better aim and let us leap into PLCs with more confidence.

How Do We Create Effective Learning Environments for Adults?

You are probably reading this book because you are eager to implement effective PLCs. Most people when faced with a problem or issue naturally want to jump to using effective solutions. However, problem solving is most effective when the problem and its context are more completely understood. Covey (1989) describes this as making sure our ladder is placed against the correct wall.

We believe that a deeper understanding of adult learning and change will enhance your commitment to key structural and relational practices needed in PLCs. If you understand why a variety of strategies and changes are important to your adult learners and the changes you seek, you will be better able to adjust your implementation plans, timetables, and strategies to meet the needs of learners in your specific setting. Therefore, we invite you to explore the contextual elements that influence an effective learning environment for adults. In the following sections we highlight some of the critical ideas about adult learning. For those interested in a deeper exploration, a specialized reference list about adult learning, change, and PLCs can be found in the Reference section.

Adult learning has received increasing attention because our information age society requires continuous learning and change, whereas the old industrial age society required "one time" career training that prepared a person for life. If teachers are to change throughout their careers, adult educators and leaders need to know what practices will influence and facilitate change in adults.

In general, research identifies five key adult learning needs:

1. Adult learners need to learn through experience within a real setting or context.

2. Learning for adults is socially transacted, negotiated, relationship-based, and collaborative.

3. A key difference between adult learning and pedagogy is that adults prefer self-directed learning.

4. There is wide agreement that adults need to participate in individual or group reflection on their learning.

5. There is also an increasing awareness of the need to learn in a community of learners.

For professional learning to be effective, educators must perceive that their learning opportunity results in beneficial changes in their practice that also lead to increases in student learning. What helps educators perceive this change?

Rosenholtz (1991) studied the organization of schools and found four factors led to perceived effective learning opportunities. These factors were the extent to which principals and teachers developed the same instructional goals, the extent to which principal evaluations were imbedded in teachers' goal setting and provided specific feedback and assistance, the extent of shared goals about teaching, and the extent of teacher collaboration. Foord (2004) investigated practices in a PLC that influenced changes in beliefs and practices and were considered transformative by participants. Identified practices included a focus on professional teaching standards, social construction of meaning, reflective practice, and self-directed learning.

As schools design effective adult environments within their PLCs, we encourage attention to four commonly agreed on characteristics: experiential learning; transactional, negotiated, relational, or collaborative learning; self-directed learning; and reflective learning. Understanding these important characteristics can guide effective implementation of learning communities. A brief explanation of each of the characteristics follows.

Experiential Learning

Effective adult learning is characterized by the use of personal experience as a key learning resource. However, not all experience educates and, in fact, some experience *mis*-educates. Simply putting teachers together in a group to share experiences will not assure effective learning from experience. As one principal we know explained, "Sometimes educators don't know what they don't know and yet they keep doing what they've always done by sharing old strategies that didn't work before." Obviously, the quality of the experience matters.

Educators can improve learning through experience if they develop skills to tap experiences. Kolb (1984) suggests that adult learning through experience requires "four abilities: an openness and willingness to involve oneself in new experiences (concrete experience); observational and reflective skills so these new experiences can be viewed from a variety of perspectives (reflective observation); analytical abilities so integrative ideas and concepts can be created from their observations (abstract conceptualization); and decision-making and problem-solving skills so these new ideas and concepts can be used in actual practice (active experimentation)" (Merriam & Cafferella, 1999, p. 224).

If teachers are to use their experience to guide learning in PLCs, they will need skills in observation, reflection, analysis, integration, decision making, problem solving, and planning, as well as dispositions favorable to openness and willingness to try new experiences. We know of no schools where a systematic preassessment of teacher readiness to learn from experience has been conducted much less used to develop teacher capacity to use experiences as key resources for learning. Assuring that teachers have or develop these skills and dispositions will increase the effectiveness of experiential learning.

Experiential learning also involves the emotions or feelings attached to prior experiences. Just as students find learning difficult when negative emotions are present, educators must work

> Habit-bound thinking can limit even the best PLC if new experiences are not introduced to change perceptions.

through any negative feelings to set them aside while retaining and enhancing positive feelings. Feelings of fear about the potential impact of a new innovation, such as PLCs, often rest in negative feelings associated with past experiences. If we ignore the negative emotions of past experiences, access to new learning will be blocked. In one school we found it helpful to shift the negative emotional tone by changing the metaphor used in the setting. The metaphor that had prevailed was one of defending the castle from invasion. Suggestions for change from the state, district office, or other schools were referred to as "bombs lobbed over the wall." This war metaphor was replaced by the picture of an exciting river rafting trip to encourage collaboration with navigating the rapids of change together. As leaders, we need to place our teachers in a learning process that feels safe yet challenging, one that recognizes both meaning and emotions. We need to construct settings that shift attention to the learners' experiences and that also address their feelings about those experiences to assure effective, positive engagement in learning.

The sheer length, breadth, and depth of adult experiences can both enrich and prevent learning. Knowles et al. (1984) explain that "adults are themselves the richest resources for one another. But there is a possible negative consequence. Because of their experience, adults often have developed habitual ways of thinking and acting, preconceptions about reality, prejudices, and defensiveness about their past ways of thinking and doing" (p. 10). Habit-bound thinking can limit even the best PLC if new experiences are not introduced to change perceptions. Adults like learning activities to be problem centered and to be meaningful to their life situations. "Adults do not learn for the sake of learning; they learn in order to be able to perform a task, solve a problem, or live in a more satisfying way" (Knowles et al., 1984, p. 12). Past experiences affect current learning and are linked to the adult's self-concept. Adults tend toward self-directedness in their learning (Brookfield, 1986).

Effective experiential learning in PLCs builds skills and processes by which experience becomes learning, pays attention to feelings and emotions, and focuses the learning on problems in real life in a specific setting.

Social, Transactional, Negotiated, Relational, Collaborative Learning

Adults learn best when they are allowed to share their understanding with others through discussion. When adults share their knowledge and beliefs they construct a negotiated, shared, and deeper understanding of their practices. Learning is most effective when the learner is challenged by a mentor who poses a challenge slightly higher than the cognitive level of the learner. In collaborative learning settings, adults serve as mutual mentors challenging this zone of proximal development for each other (Vygotsky, 1978). Fullan (2002) believes that "shared expertise is the driver of instructional change, and . . . good ideas come from talented people working together" (p. 19). Effective educators negotiate priorities, methods, assessments, and evaluative criteria. As they do so "dissension and criticism are regarded as inevitable and desirable elements of the process" (Brookfield, 1986, p. 24).

Why is social dialogue so important to adult learning? Peter Senge (1995) explains that "learning organizations are spaces for generative conversations and concerted action. In them, language functions as a device for connections, invention, and coordination. . . Dialogue weaves a common fabric and connects [people] at a deep level of being" (p. 50). Creating this aligned, engaging dialogue takes skill and practice.

Simply placing teachers in groups will not produce aligned dialogue, healthy transactions, or effective, collaborative relationships. Interpersonal communication, conflict resolution, and group processing skills must be an integral part of the learning by adults to assure PLC success. "Collaboration must be taught, learned, nurtured, and supported until it replaces working privately" (Lieberman, Saxl, & Miles, 1988, p. 156). Collaborative inquiry is the major role of educators in PLCs. In our experience, leaders incorrectly assume the presence of these skills when they are largely absent. When these skills are missing, we have seen PLCs solidify into either open, competitive conflict or cold, defensive silence.

Self-Directed Learning

Adults need to be involved in the planning and evaluation of their learning to ensure its immediate value in their adult life. When adults are directed in their actions by others, resentment and resistance can arise. Knowles, Holton, and Swanson (1998) suggest,

> [T]he point at which an individual achieves a self-concept of essential self-direction is the point at which he psychologically becomes adult . . . The individual develops a deep psychological need to be perceived by others as be-

ing self-directing. Thus, when he finds himself in a situation in which he is not allowed to be self-directing, he experiences a tension between that situation and his self-concept. His reaction is bound to be tainted with resentment and resistance. (p. 56)

Healthy adults resist being treated as objects to be used by someone and strive as much as possible to control what occurs in their learning environment.

How important is self-direction to the educators in your learning environment? Does external direction seem to breed resentment and resistance? What conditions will foster more conscious, complex, self-direction by your educators? How can we assure that self-direction doesn't lead to unresponsive, independent contractors?

As leaders who understand the importance of self-direction in building commitment to change, we need to think about how to balance direction and self-direction in PLCs. This goes well beyond the "tight versus loose" control (DuFour et al., 1998) to issues of adult identity, responsibility, change, and resistance. One principal we know puzzled over the "tight versus loose" control issue when she entered a new school. When she reflected on the needs of the adult learners in her school, she resolved that she would expect clear documentation of teacher learning to increase specific professional standards but left it up to her teachers to determine the content, form, and evidence for the learning.

Reflective Learning

Reflection is the process of inquiry into one's beliefs and practices that involves commitment to continuous learning and improvement (York-Barr, Sommers, Ghere, & Montie, 2001). Through reflection, adults commit to both problem finding and problem solving as part of the reflective process. Reflection leads to making judgments about the impact of change on oneself, other people, or entire systems. Reflection also results in some form of action even if the action is a deliberate choice not to change (Merriam & Caffarella, 1999).

Reflection can focus on past actions, on future actions, or on current actions (Schon, 1987a). When past actions are analyzed, potential changes for future actions are revealed. Reflection while in action is the most difficult to perform but allows educators to make ongoing decisions to adjust practices while teaching or during meetings.

If PLCs are to produce changes in practice, assumptions must be challenged. Adults will choose consistency to old practices that support their assumptions over commitment to new practices that are contrary to assumptions (Cialdini, 2007). Reflection supports analysis, confirmation, or rejection of assumptions. Critical, collaborative reflection on experiences is "one of the most significant forms of adult learning in which individuals can engage" (Brookfield, 1986, p. 98). This process is strengthened when we involve other people in examining ideas and actions in new ways. When professional standards are used as an external reference point to examine teacher beliefs and practices, unexamined assumptions that might prevent change are more effectively surfaced. The external reference point also provides a target for positive change. In a year-long PLC we facilitated, teachers explained that reflection on profession standards (Danielson, 1996) and the practices they used that were aligned to these standards was a key motivation for high levels of change in practices.

Within PLCs, critical analysis of our own perspectives, including our emotions, hopes, dreams, and experiences, leads to a transformative sense of responsibility and appreciation for additional perspectives. According to Mezirow (2000) reflection supports the transformation of perspective through ten phases: (a) a disorienting dilemma; (b) self-examination of feelings; (c) critical assessment of assumptions; (d) recognition that one's discontent and the process of transformation are shared with others; (e) exploration of options for new roles, relationships, and actions; (f) planning a course of action; (g) acquiring knowledge of skills for implementing one's plan; (h) provisional trying of new roles; (i) building confidence and self confidence in the new roles and relationships; (j) reintegration into one's life on the basis of conditions dictated by one's new perspective" (p. 22). Typically, educators who are placed into groups jump from the first phase, a disorienting dilemma, to the sixth phase, planning a course of action. Feelings, values, assumptions, shared experiences, purposes, roles, relationships, or possible actions are not explored, but will most assuredly appear later, usually as disagreements or outright conflicts. All ten phases should be considered when implementing PLCs. As we have worked with schools on the implementation of PLCs, we have been able to observe firsthand the significant transformation of practices by those groups who were attentive to these phases.

Reflective learning not only allows for a closer analysis of assumptions and perceptions, it also allows for an analysis of teaching practices. Several authors have designed various means to encourage reflection in practice. Systematic reflection through peer coaching was introduced through cognitive coaching by Costa and Garmston

> Within professional learning communities, critical analysis of our own perspectives, including our emotions, hopes, dreams, and experiences leads to a transformative sense of responsibility and appreciation for additional perspectives.

(2002). Coaching conversations can encourage reflection, planning, or problem solving. Various protocols have also been developed by Glickman (2002) and the Annenberg Foundation (2002) to guide reflection on classroom lessons and student work. York-Barr et al. (2001) offer strategies for reflection at all levels of the educational system, starting with self-reflection and ending with reflection as a school district. Coaching, protocols, and reflective practice strategies, when applied, can facilitate aligned construction of meaning by educators and leaders as they change practices.

One last consideration involving reflective learning is that reflection in groups may be a primary way of increasing learning and efficacy for female educators. Dialogue and storytelling develops the authoritative "voice" that solidifies what we understand to be our reality (Fivush, 2000). Research on reflection by women (Belinky & Stanton, 2000) shows a preference for connected ways of knowing through dialogue rather than individual subjective ways of knowing. Because women represent a majority of educators in some schools, this feminist perspective is an important consideration for leaders.

Reflective learning is supported in a professional community where individuals and groups process their learning through critical reflection. Ongoing inquiry into beliefs and practices leads to transformation, collective efficacy, authoritative voice, and commitment to continuous learning and improvement.

How Do We Influence Change in Teachers' Beliefs and Practices?

Adults' learning needs must be considered in the design and implementation of PLCs, but there are also several essential ideas about change that should guide our thinking and work. Much of the change that has been thrust on schools has involved changing goals, roles, rules, structures, or measurements. Change is often treated as a measurable product rather than an ongoing process involving significant changes in culture. This ignores the role of social structures in the change process that are embedded in systems of meaning, value, belief, and knowledge. "To change an organization's structure, one must attend not only to rules, roles, and relationships but to systems of beliefs, values, and knowledge" (Evans, 1996, p. 17). Helping others "see" the systems of social structures is a challenge.

Cultures within organizations, explain Bolman and Deal (1997), work to preserve the status quo and resist imposed change. Sergiovanni (1996) observed that "the change strategies we choose are a function of our mindscapes [beliefs] about schools" (p. 157). When strategies fail, educators and the public tend to seek explanations and solutions within the same old paradigms instead of searching within new paradigms. Professional learning communities can support two changes in perspectives that will leverage school improvement. First, change should be viewed as capacity building, "enabling and empowering teachers by increasing their skills and increasing their commitment to professional values" (Sergiovanni, 1996, p. 140). Second, change should be viewed as systems-changing, where professionals explore what is effective and schools are viewed as communities, not organizations.

In most models of school change teachers are the central figures. However, "school improvement faces a fierce paradox: its essential agents of change—teachers—are also its targets and, sometimes, its foes" (Evans, 1996, p. xii). Changes must match the individual and cultural beliefs as well as the context and purposes of the principle change agents—the teachers.

When attempts are made to change belief structures, the response to change is determined by how the change is understood, by how it affects prior attachments and beliefs, and by how people make sense of how the change fits into their existing and future world. Evans (1996) argues that

> When the ultimate goal is a change in beliefs and assumptions, something that cannot be imposed, it is often necessary to insist on a change in behavior, which can be. Changes in behavior lead to, as well as flow from changes in belief. . . Simply imposing change stiffens resistance . . . [while] experimenting with a new behavior is often a prerequisite to acquiring new learning. (p. 71)

Hall and Hord (2001) have demonstrated that the success of change is dependent on the level of use of a new practice by an educator. Implementation moves from no use, to routine use, and eventually to collaborative adaptations to improve practice. They developed a system called the Concerns Based Adoption Model (CBAM) to help assess the stages of concern that surface on the affective side of change. Change processes must attend to people's reactions, feelings, perceptions, and attitudes. This is facilitated by sharing awareness and information about the change, encouraging personal management of new learning and practices, and collaborating to improve the success of current and future changes.

Significant changes in teacher' attitudes and beliefs come after they have had an opportunity to apply new practices and see the results of their changes

> Changes in practices lead to changes in beliefs.

translated into improvements in student achievement. Changes in practices can lead to changes in beliefs; however, teachers' initial beliefs and assumptions in key areas also influence the degree of change. The degree to which a change is integrated into practice, according to Toole (2001) is shaped by teachers' assumptions or beliefs about five core areas: student cognitive development, student self regulation, teacher social relations, application of learning by teachers, and personal teacher efficacy. In recent research, McLaughlin and Talbert (2006) found that effective PLC implementation was shaped by teachers' beliefs about students, the role of the learner, curriculum, instruction, and assessment practices, professionalism and professional relationships, and use of resources.

Stigler and Hiebert (1999) identified six principles needed for effective change in teacher beliefs and practices. Figure 2.1 shows how each principle can be addressed in a PLC.

Figure 2.1. Principles for Change in the Learning Community

Change Principle	Learning Community Strategies
Expect improvement to be continual, gradual, and incremental	Community works together for one year, sharing efforts and successes each week
Maintain a constant focus on student learning goals	Student understanding and performance are measured pre and post as well as in an ongoing formative fashion
Focus on teaching, not teachers	Danielson's Framework or National Board of Professional Teaching Standards are used as the criteria to discuss and improve teaching
Make improvements in context	Teams select an action project to focus learning and application in their own classes
Make improvements in the work of teachers	Select research based practices to improve teaching and structure systems that permit sharing among teachers
Build a system that can learn from its own experience	Use weekly reflection, sharing, and planning to reinforce learning

The make-up of the staff in a school also bears attention when considering how to structure changes. According to Evans (1996) schools are faced with a majority of staff who are middle-aged and whose characteristics contribute to resistance to change. The typical middle-aged teacher faces mid-life changes including: aging parents, children of their own, and a point of stability if not stagnation in their teaching development.

Stability in teaching is characterized by a lack of motivation for diminished rewards, a view of work as less challenging and interesting, a marked loss of feedback on performance, and growing isolation from peers. Stability in teaching can shift to sustained, positive growth by finding ways to develop strengths, celebrate successes, appreciate achievements, and share what is learned with others (Evans, 1996). New norms or incentives for professional learning may be needed in addition to professional standards for effective practice to assure ongoing change for experienced teachers. In one school district with a large proportion of seasoned teachers, the superintendent and board of education added a new lane in the salary schedule to encourage teachers to seek National Board of Teaching certification or seek a certificate at a local college to improve their data driven, decision-making skills. One of the authors delighted in the professional transformation of a seasoned team member when she coauthored a grant that required extensive new learning and co-teaching using technology in the classroom.

Replacing teacher stability with professional growth and replacing teacher isolation with collaborative professional relationships is essential to long-term change. Hargreaves (1994) and Lieberman et al. (1988) contend that teacher isolation as a norm needs to be replaced with collegiality. Through professional collegiality, teachers obtain a sense of reward from adult relationships as well as student relationships. Barth (1989) observes that "although collegiality's benefits are obvious, logical, and compelling, it is the least common form of relationship among adults in schools" (pp. 229–230). When teachers are engaged in long-term, collaborative, and intellectually challenging PLCs, they develop the trust needed to question traditional beliefs and assumptions required for lasting change.

What does effective change look like in a PLC? A visual model of the change process for adult learners (Figure 2.2) developed by Foord (2004) was adapted from the work of McCarthy and Leflar (1983). McCarthy and Leflar integrated learning styles with the six stages of concern in the CBAM by Hall and Hord (2001) to help professional trainers assure effective changes from new learning.

The change cycle portrays the intersection of two dimensions of learning—perceiving and processing—which results in four different learning styles: concrete experience, reflective observation, abstract conceptualization, and active experimentation. This intersection is based on the work of Kolb (1984), who described the perceiving dimension as moving from sensing/feeling to thinking, whereas the processing dimension moved from acting to watching. Kolb called the sensing/feeling dimension "concrete experience," the watching dimension "reflective observation," the thinking dimension "abstract conceptualization," and the acting/doing dimension "active experimentation." Traditional professional development has focused almost exclusively on the thinking dimension by engaging teachers in training "events" with an occasional application of learning in the classroom to move teachers into the acting/doing dimension. Limited attention has been given to the sensing/feeling or watching dimensions where experience and critical reflection are also used to create more effective learning. Because experiential and reflective learning are critical to adult learning, the failure to include these practices in professional development has long limited effective adult learning. In one learning community, we found that teachers who indicated a preference for learning through thinking and doing, shifted to a preference for reflection on experiences after following the change cycle model for a year.

> Replacing teacher stability with professional growth and replacing teacher isolation with collaborative professional relationships is essential to long-term change. Teacher isolation as a norm needs to be replaced with collegiality.

The cycle of learning demonstrated in this model moves learners from experience into concepts and then translates concepts into experience in a never-ending process that helps educators make meaning.

Figure 2.2. Change Cycle

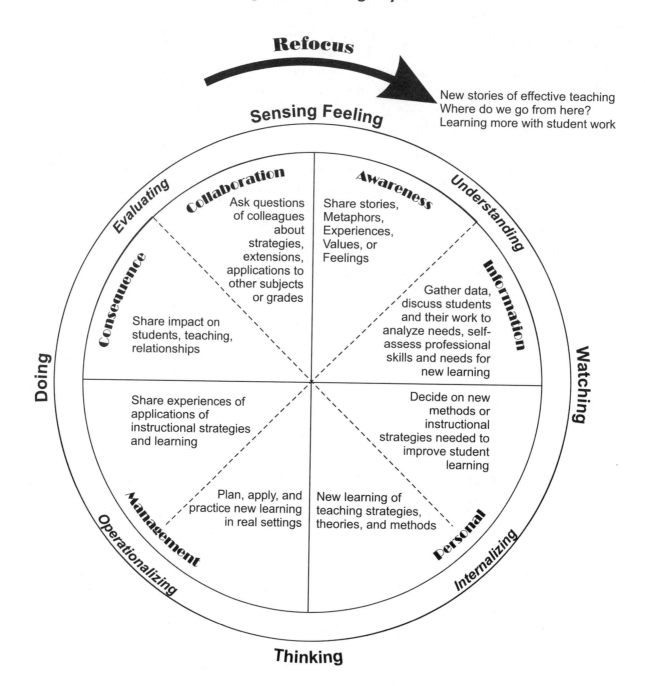

Let's use Figure 2.2, to see how change would appear in a PLC. Change begins at the top of the figure in the "understanding" quadrant (awareness and information) by educators developing awareness through shared stories, perceptions, and experiences. At the awareness stage it is important to develop understanding of issues or problems through shared construction of meaning and definitions. Metaphors are especially effective in developing a deep, shared understanding of issues or problems. For example, teachers in our learning communities who have explained the metaphors "Effective education is ..." or "Effective learning is ..." have created a deeper understanding of the issues around determining and defining "effective education" and "effective learning." They have also been able to identify component parts and interrelationships among parts of the issues.

Some schools skip this awareness step and jump into the information analysis stage, using data to drive home the importance of predetermined changes. In our experience, when the data did not match the awareness or perceptions of teachers, the data was dismissed by teachers as biased, false, unrepresentative, or insufficient. When teachers have been invited to collect and analyze data about student and teacher learning in line with their prior awareness or perceptions, they have been more receptive to data that challenged their assumptions and practices. The role of the leader is to shape discussions in the initial stage to surface awareness of issues or problems involving student and teacher learning.

In the information stage, the leader provides access to data from multiple sources and facilitates analysis of the data. Data sources can include achievement scores or ratings, but should also address demographic, perception, and school process data (Bernhardt, 2005). During this stage, educators must analyze both student learning data and teacher learning data to determine not only what student learning is needed, but what new professional learning is needed. When student learning data is the sole source of information, the emphasis is on changing students not on changing teaching. This typically creates a condition where the student is blamed for deficits in learning. Student learning data must be interpreted for changes needed in teaching, thereby shifting the responsibility, ownership, and commitment for improved learning to improvements in teaching. These changes in teaching become the focus of new professional learning in a PLC.

> When student learning data is the sole source of information, the emphasis is on changing students not on changing teaching. Student learning data must be interpreted for changes needed in teaching, thereby shifting the responsibility, ownership, and commitment for improved learning to improvements in teaching.

In the "internalizing" quadrant (personal), new learning must also align to best practices in curriculum, instruction, and assessment to meet student learning needs identified in the awareness and information stages. Allowing sufficient time for internalization produces teacher commitment to new learning. We have witnessed PLCs fail when central administration has insisted on commitment to new learning without involving teachers and principals in understanding the need for the new learning. Teachers readily learn new theories, strategies, and methods when they are committed to the importance of this learning.

In the "operationalizing" quadrant (management), learning is reinforced through application and practice in real settings. Adult learners must self-direct this new application and personally experience the impact of the new learning in their own classrooms or settings. Attempts to foolproof the application process with strictly proscribed lessons dictated at the district level stops the learning process. Sharing successes and concerns during implementation permits teachers to socially construct understanding about the correct use of the new learning. This stage operationalizes change by helping teachers learn to direct and manage the implementation of the new learning.

In the final stage of change, the "evaluating" quadrant (consequences and collaboration), teachers evaluate the consequences of their learning and action by sharing the impact on students, themselves, and the learning system. They also collaborate to improve the application of new learning by sharing strategies that worked and discussing ways to alter strategies that did not work. This reflective conversation quite naturally refocuses awareness and perceptions for new needs, issues, or problems, thus starting the cycle of learning all over again.

The change-cycle process honors a variety of adult learning needs at each stage and addresses all adult learning needs during the entire process. The process can be used at the district, school, department, or smaller PLC level to guide the professional learning process. Professional learning community meetings may need to focus on a single stage at a time. At other times, a single meeting may encompass all stages in the process.

In one highly effective PLC, participants met once a month after school for three hours. During the first hour, they shared stories about their application of new strategies, and they examined the corresponding student work. During the second hour, participants learned new strategies aligned to increasing their competence in selected professional standards. During the third hour, participants met in smaller, self-directed teams to plan how they would apply their new learning or extend the use of previous strategies they had learned. Once a week, the small teams met for one hour to reflect on their new application of learning. Sometimes they scheduled observations in each other's classrooms to see how the application worked in another setting. The smaller, self-directed teams determined what they would share at their next large PLC meeting and what questions they might ask of members in their larger community of learners. This pattern resulted in significant professional growth and personal satisfaction with learning in a PLC.

What Conditions Are Needed for an Effective Professional Learning Community?

Professional learning communities are becoming a desired change structure caused in large part by the work of DuFour and Eaker (1998). They argue that the following characteristics are essential for PLC development: (a) shared mission, vision, values, and goals; (b) collective inquiry; (c) collaborative teams; (d) action orientation and experimentation; (e) continuous improvement; and (f) results orientation. They also suggest that tight control over mission, vision, values, goals, and results will permit looser control over the other characteristics. Hundreds of schools and educators are implementing PLCs using these practices as their guides. However, there are several other voices in the field of PLCs that we believe deserve our attention. Figure 2.3 summarizes the authors' perspectives. We also share brief explanations of the authors' views. We invite you to note the similarities and differences in characteristics deemed essential for PLCs.

Figure 2.3. Authors' Perspectives on Essential Characteristics of Professional Learning Communities

Author(s)	Perspective
DuFour & Eaker (1998)	Tight vs. loose control
Collay, Dunlap, Enloe, & Gagne (1998)	Stages and conditions
Bransford, Brown, & Cocking (2000)	Centered foci
Louis, Kruse, & Bryk (1995)	Structural and social supports
Toole (2001)	Ways we think and ways we interact
Sergiovanni (1994)	Four commitments
McLaughlin & Talbert (2006)	Technical culture, professional norms, organizational policies
Goddard, Hoy, & Hoy (2004)	Collective capability and efficacy
Little (1990), Hargreaves (1994)	Authentic collegiality
Hord (2004)	Leadership actions and support
Johnson, Johnson, & Smith (2006)	Cooperative learning

Collay et al. (1998) explain that PLCs progress through five stages of development (initiating, forming, maintaining, sustaining, and transforming) and require six conditions. The six conditions are building community, constructing knowledge, supporting learners, documenting reflection, assessing expectations, and changing cultures. Similar categories were identified by Bransford et al. (2000) who suggested that adult learning communities must be learner-centered, knowledge-centered, assessment-centered, and community-centered.

According to Louis et al. (1995), structural and social supports for PLCs include shared values, reflective dialogue, deprivatization of practice, focus on student learning, and collaboration. Structural conditions that enhance community involve support for communication and teacher empowerment, whereas social and human resources that enhance community involve supportive leadership, socialization, openness to learning and expertise, and conditions of trust and respect.

Toole (2001) defines beliefs in community as "ways we think" with effective thinking involving systems thinking, shared purpose, collective focus on student learning, innovation orientation, and collective responsibility. He defines practices in community as "ways we interact" with effective practices including collaboration, team learning, staff development, and reflective dialogue.

Sergiovanni (1994) explains that it is the web of relationships that stands out in a learning situation, and it is the quality and character of the relationships that shape the values, beliefs, norms, and practices of the learners. He argues that a learning community increases professionalism by creating

> It is the web of relationships that stands out in a learning situation, and it is the quality and character of the relationships that shape the values, beliefs, norms, and practices of the learners.

four commitments: to practice in an exemplary way, to practice toward valued social ends, to commit to one's practice and the practice itself, and to practice an ethic of caring.

McLaughlin and Talbert (2006) reviewed 15 years of research on PLCs and found that teacher professional communities differ from one another in three ways:

- ◆ Technical culture: views of students, conceptions of subject content, beliefs about student learning, and understanding of effective pedagogy and assessment
- ◆ Professional norms: collegial relations, views of professional expertise, and conceptions of career
- ◆ Organizational policies: criteria for course or class assignments and resource allocation, for example. (p. 18)

McLaughlin and Talbert also explain how collective capacity develops in PLCs:

Questions change as teachers assume norms of collective responsibility and a service of ethic, moving from questions centered on an individual teachers competence to assessments of community capacity: What is this faculty going to do about disappointing student outcomes? About significant achievement differences among groups of students? When this happens, ongoing learning and critical reflection become professional norms; practice synchronizes because teachers have clear, shared understandings of one another's classroom work. Understandings about collective responsibility promote collective growth. They also allow collective autonomy, or teachers' ability to act on their professional best judgment as they work with their students in their classrooms, because community norms and expectations are clearly understood. (p. 9)

Some proponents of PLCs suggest that if teachers commit to tightly controlled school goals and to increased student achievement they will naturally develop collective efficacy and make effective, collaborative, instructional decisions. However, Goddard et al. (2004) found that "schools that formally turn over instructionally relevant school decisions to teachers tend to have higher levels of perceived collective efficacy. Collective efficacy beliefs, in turn, foster commitment to school goals and gains in student achievement" (p. 10). They found that "even after controlling for students' prior achievement, race/ethnicity, socioeconomic status (SES), and gender, collective efficacy beliefs have stronger effects on student achievement than student race or SES. Teachers' beliefs about the collective capability of their faculty vary greatly among schools and are strongly linked to student achievement" (p. 7). In other words, when we systematically develop the awareness of our teachers about their collective capability, the increase in their collective efficacy will have a strong impact on student achievement.

Little (1990) also found that a focus on collegiality had a strong relationship to an increased ability to examine and apply new ideas, methods, and materials resulting in gains in student achievement and increased professional confidence. However, Hargreaves (1994) warns against contrived, bureaucratically imposed collegiality that stifles teachers collaborative efforts because it lacks a central purpose agreed on by the participants for directing their own improvement. An authentic mentoring community sustains teacher commitment through deep, formative dialogue and reflection.

> An authentic mentoring community sustains teacher commitment through deep, formative dialogue and reflection.

Hord (2004) has explored the principal's role in promoting effective PLCs. She found that "in the creation of PLCs, not only were a principal's actions crucial but also teachers' perceptions of his/her actions. These perceptions determine teachers' willingness to support principal's actions. Without a willingness on the part of teachers, it is highly unlikely that schools can develop into professional learning communities." (p. 45)

Hord identified five dimensions of leadership that are crucial in the development of PLCs.

1. Developing collective values and vision—this includes becoming student focused and using the vision to develop/recruit quality staff;

2. Supporting shared decision-making—this includes establishing structures/processes for shared decision-making, promoting shared decision-making on substantive issues, and increasing decision-making capacity;

3. Promoting continuous learning—including communicating the value of learning, monitoring growth and progress, and connecting professional development to school improvement goals;

4. Encouraging collaboration—by providing time/support for collaboration and identifying outcomes of collaboration;

5. Providing support—by establishing clear expectations, developing relationships, devising structures for communication, and acknowledging the human capacity for change.

As school leaders, we are faced with many variables and conditions in the implementation of PLCs. Our understanding of the perspectives of a wide variety of authors will help us respond more effectively to the specific needs of our educators in our settings.

How Do We Promote Effective Relationships in Professional Learning Communities?

Much of the research mentioned earlier has recognized the importance of interpersonal relationships in effective PLCs. It cannot be assumed that individuals know how to interact effectively. Hackman (cited in York-Barr et al., 2001) found that groups who get off to a good start got increasingly better, and those that got off to a poor start remained poor. Teachers must develop interpersonal and conflict management skills to deal with the discomfort of change necessary to effective learning in PLCs.

We believe that this important aspect of PLCs needs much more emphasis than it has received in the past. Leaders can increase relational practices by teaching, guiding, and expecting cooperative learning conditions within PLCs. Cooperative learning has long been used as an effective means to create classroom environments that foster student achievement, enhanced motivation, increased self-esteem, and positive interpersonal communication (Johnson et al., 2006). Applying the conditions for effective cooperative learning to the development of relational capacity in PLCs can accelerate the development of collective action and efficacy among teachers. Teachers who have not worked collaboratively may ignore many of these essential conditions. Each condition is needed to produce effective learning and change. The conditions are (a) interdependence of roles, responsibilities, and goals; (b) face to face interaction; (c) effective interpersonal interaction; (d) effective group processing; and (e) individual and group accountability. The relevance of these relational practices in

PLCs as well as a comparison between practices of cooperative learning and practices in PLCs will be discussed more fully in Chapter 5.

Post Vignette

Teresa invited two principals in the district to join her as they tackled learning about PLCs. In doing so they formed their own principal PLC. Together they wanted to learn more about how adults learn and change, how to implement the characteristics and strategies needed for high functioning PLCs, how to develop effective relationships among adult learners, and how to help adults make interdependent decisions for continuous improvement. They selected several texts and divided up the work. The principals summarized their learning and suggested how the learning could be applied in their own settings as they developed PLCs. Together they reflected on the various information, theories, strategies, and practices. They collaborated to develop working documents of the information and then suggested professional development models and strategies that could be used in their respective schools as they implemented PLCs.

Teresa reflected with her principal PLC about the needs of adults in her setting. They needed to be more self directed, reflect on how their practices aligned with professional standards, and involve plenty of time to construct meaning with one another about the changes needed. She now understood that change was incremental, and she needed to plan for stages of change that involved revisiting and refocusing on what was learned from experience and practice. The members of her principal PLC were amazed that any learning or change had occurred in the past with all the missteps they had promoted.

Teresa started to think about how she might help her teachers develop more awareness about professional standards for teaching and the diverse needs of their student population. What was their purpose as educators? What experiences would help them construct and reflect on this awareness? What questions could she ask to help teachers seek data or information to confirm or challenge this new awareness? Teresa began to understand that her key role as a leader was to guide her teachers to their own understanding through questions, experiences, and reflection. Her job now was to sift through all this new learning and compose questions and determine experiences that would allow her teachers to answer those questions.

Vignette Analysis

Through shared work in her principal PLC, Teresa has gained significant new insights about adult learning, change, and PLCs. She is more committed to self-directed learning, reflection, and socially constructed meaning about professional practices. She understands that change is a process that is incremental and starts with building shared awareness. She has developed her own awareness of the broader field of PLC research. Teresa has discovered the power of questions and understands that her key role is to develop and use them. She understands better how to approach both her adult learners and the change process to develop collective efficacy and support for PLCs. Indeed, her own confidence has increased because she took the time to develop collective efficacy for the change process with her principal colleagues. Teresa examined her assumptions about adult learners, change, and PLCs and has expanded her own awareness so that she is now ready to seek information and data about the needs of her teachers and students. These are good beginning steps in preparation for leading the effective implementation of PLCs.

Reflecting Forward

As you reflect on the content shared in Chapter 2, on Teresa's situation with implementing PLCs, and on your situation with PLC implementation, we ask you to reflect on the following questions:

- ♦ Which adult learning principles and practices are present in your setting?
- ♦ Which elements of effective change practices are present in your setting?
- ♦ How does the change cycle suggested in this chapter compare with that used in your setting?
- ♦ How would you characterize relational practices in your setting?

Chapter Wrap-Up

We continue to investigate the conditions and characteristics required in effective PLCs in our research with schools and offer our ideas about essential practices in the rest of the book. In Chapter 1 and Chapter 2 we have focused on an increase in awareness of underlying assumptions, theories, and principles that impact PLC development. We hope the information increases your commitment to learning and implementing new practices for effective, sustainable PLCs. In the remaining chapters we will move through the quadrants in the change-cycle model as you learn, plan, and apply techniques, and then reflect, evaluate, and collaborate with your staff to improve the implementation of PLCs.

3

Using Innovation Maps to Guide Implementation

Vignette 3

Because of her own professional growth through a principal PLC, Teresa viewed PLCs as a positive process for honoring adult and student learning. It provided her with a natural, respectful way to lead teacher and student growth. The challenge came with providing a clear picture of what needed to change. How could she help teachers examine information and evidence that would inspire a commitment to necessary changes? How could she be attentive to the turbulence and confusion her teachers were experiencing while also being attentive to the obvious need to make changes that would increase student achievement? Teresa was meeting with her leadership team later in the day. She planned to share with them the documents, the professional development models and the strategies she had developed in her principal PLC. By using the documents, models, and strategies as resources, she would initiate conversations to address her concerns. Teresa knew her leadership team well enough to know the conversations would result in specific plans for their school's PLCs.

Guiding Questions

- How do we develop commitment to a common purpose in PLCs?
- How can we assess student learning?
- How can we determine if professional growth is improving student learning?
- How do we know what needs to change to improve student learning and teacher learning?

How Do We Develop Commitment to a Common Purpose in Professional Learning Communities?

A common purpose of PLCs is to develop the means to address change. Dennis Sparks (2005) notes, "Well-implemented PLCs are a powerful means of seamlessly blending teaching and professional learning in ways that produce complex, intelligent behavior in all teachers" (p. 9). Within a well-implemented PLC, teachers strengthen their knowledge and skill about teaching and learning; they learn to communicate and share the knowledge and skills among themselves as well as with others; and they implement the knowledge and skills in a manner that is focused on improving student learning.

Leadership matters in sustaining change through PLCs. Leaders play a key role not only in monitoring the progress of PLCs but also in actively promoting collaborative changes in instruction, curriculum, and assessment—changes that for some teachers come after years of isolated practice. As school leaders, we establish a collective understanding of the process of change through PLCs. We guide our teachers as they assess our school's effectiveness with teaching and learning and as they determine changes needed. Guidance through the steps in the process aids in a clear understanding of the purpose and value of PLCs, making change more probable.

> Leaders play a key role not only in monitoring the progress of PLCs but also in actively promoting collaborative changes in instruction, curriculum and assessment—changes that for some teachers come after years of isolated practice.

Leaders can use assessment to clarify a collective understanding of the purpose of PLCs and to determine an entry point for making needed changes. Providing time and a process for teacher understanding of assessment information is crucial to teacher buy-in. Understanding is enhanced when teachers and leaders use a variety of evidence to examine achievement, perception, demographic, and school-process data. Data is analyzed not only for student learning but also for teacher learning that is needed.

In one school district, teachers completed a self-assessment using Danielson's framework (1996) to indicate areas of competence where they felt they most needed to grow. Leaders used the results to focus professional development and coaching on 10 key elements instead of trying to coach teachers on all 66 elements. In another district, the principals selected eight elements for focus based on their analysis of evaluative observations from the previous year. In a middle school, the leadership team studied achievement, perception, demographic, and school process data and then led the entire staff in small group meetings to observe patterns in the data. Inferential reading surfaced as a key focus not only because students needed to improve, but because teachers indicated that they lacked strategies for teaching inferential reading. Their data also indicated that they needed a process for sharing the skills of their reading specialist with teachers on their staff. Unified commitment to applying new skills resulted the following year because teachers determined their purpose for learning by using data.

As leaders it is our responsibility to guide teachers as they assess their beliefs and teaching practices. Collaboratively, we examine teaching and learning styles among teachers; we develop norms and establish decision making or meeting processes; and we guide discussions to develop a collective understanding of beliefs about teaching and learning. Information garnered from these processes as well as data collected about student learning allow us to accurately assess our school, our student needs, and our need to change.

This level of commitment to common purpose requires strong knowledge and skills about teaching and learning. Any leader wanting to implement and sustain effective PLCs has to have a solid foundation in instructional leadership. This book could not possibly cover all the knowledge and skills needed by an instructional leader. We have, however, found a number of resources particularly helpful in fostering understanding and analysis of teacher beliefs, student learning, and student achievement. For instance, Victoria Bernhardt's (2005) work, including such books as *Using Data to Improve Student Learning,* permits development of profiles for assessing student achievement, perception, demographic, and school-processes data to define the focus of your school improvement efforts.

Other resources that are useful in developing leadership knowledge and skills about effective teaching and learning include the following:

♦ Danielson's *Enhancing Professional Practice* (1996) describes 66 elements of effective teaching with 4 levels of performance for each element.

♦ Glickman's *Leadership for Learning* (2002) supports supervision of teachers ranging from beginner through experienced teachers and guides us in how to sequence conversations and questions to direct or encourage professional growth.

♦ Butler's *Learning and Teaching Style* (1987) and McCarthy's *The 4MAT System* (1987) and *The 4MAT Research Guide* (2002) help us understand the different styles of learning that may affect teacher learning and practice.

♦ McLaughlin and Talbert's *Building School-Based Learning Communities* (2006) helps us understand the beliefs that move teachers from weak learning communities to strong learning communities

♦ Pajak's *Honoring Diverse Teaching Styles* (2003) assists leaders in designing coaching questions and processes that match teachers' learning styles.

♦ Marzano, Pollock, and Pickering's *Classroom Instruction That Works* (2001) helps us understand research-based instructional strategies that support student learning.

We do not believe leaders can sustain effective PLCs without a personal commitment to increase knowledge and skills about teaching and learning. Prior knowledge and experience will support us as leaders as we continue to learn and grow as instructional leaders. By using the resources suggested above as a foundation, we can focus on teaching and learning that is grounded in best practices and research-based evidence.

Our role as leaders is to provide a focused environment that facilitates effective change. We need processes to define student and teacher learning, identify specific entry points, determine readiness, and plan next

> We do not believe leaders can sustain effective PLCs without a personal commitment to increase knowledge and skills about teaching and learning.

steps. With such processes in place we can, in collaboration with teachers, execute effective implementation. We developed eight innovation maps to guide the systematic implementation of effective PLCs. These eight maps provide the processes needed to analyze and evaluate implementation, continuous improvement, and sustainability.

Professional Learning Community Implementation Innovation Maps

We developed innovation maps that can guide leaders through the implementation and sustainability of PLCs by analyzing the National Staff Development Council standards (revised 2001), Killion's back-mapping model (2002), Hall and Hord's innovation configuration model (2001), Johnson, Johnson, and Holubec's (1994) cooperative learning model, research by McLaughlin and Talbert (2006) on effective PLC development and teacher beliefs, and DuFour and Eaker's (1998) PLC model. We identified concepts we believe are essential for making PLCs structurally and relationally viable and organized these concepts into innovation maps.

We developed the PLC implementation innovation maps to guide school leaders through an analysis of eight key elements that must be monitored in the development of effective PLCs. Each innovation map starts with guiding questions to help uncover assumptions as teams move across levels in the innovation. The innovation maps focus attention on important components and provide descriptions of observable behaviors for teachers and leaders at three levels of PLC implementation. The eight key elements include student learning, teacher learning, PLC development, interdependence, interpersonal interactions, group processing, individual and group accountability, and PLC sustainability.

The maps have three aspects that promote effective growth and change. First, each map has a separate set of guiding questions to assess the underlying assumptions as PLCs move from one level of implementation to the next. Second, each map provides benchmark descriptions of teacher and leader actions for several characteristics at three levels of implementation. These benchmarks permit independent analysis of implementation and help guide the development of evidence to promote movement to the next level. Lastly, the maps collectively address the structural and relational practices needed for effective, sustainable PLCs.

Beginning with this chapter, we will focus on specific innovation maps as we move through the remaining chapters of the book. In this chapter we will take a closer look at Innovation Map One—Student Learning and Growth and Innovation Map Two—Professional Learning and Growth.

We begin with these two innovation maps because they reflect the central purpose of schools and because they are so closely connected. In his book, *Learning by Heart,* Roland Barth captures the essence of the importance of student learning and teacher learning: "I've yet to see a school where the learning curves of youngsters are off the chart upward while the learning curves of the adults are off the chart downward, or a school where the learning curves of the adults were steep upward and those of the students were not. Teachers and students go hand in hand as learners—or they don't go at all" (2001, p. 23).

Research has validated the important connection between effective teaching and improved student learning. A large component of PLC work, however, has focused on student learning, without regard to teacher learning. McLaughlin and Talbert (2006) agree that improving student learning depends on teacher learning; however, they argue that the ultimate payoff of teachers' learning opportunities depends on teachers' opportunities and commitment to work together to improve instruction for the students in their school. It is not enough to teach new teaching skills. Through cooperative lifelong learning, teachers learn to engage in a collective responsibility for creating an organizational culture committed to improved instruction for all students.

The benefits to student learning gained from the effective implementation of PLCs has been identified in research cited in Chapters 1 and 2. To understand why PLCs support student learning we turn to Marzano et al. (2001) who note the single most powerful impact a school can have on student achievement is to provide students with a "guaranteed and viable curriculum" that gives students access to the same essential learning regardless of who is teaching the class. Teachers are most effective in helping all students learn when they are consistent in exactly what their students must know and be able to do as a result of the course, grade level, or unit of instruction. Professional learning communities provide teachers with a collaborative structure and process to make informed and cohesive decisions about instruction, curriculum and assessment.

How Can We Assess Student Learning?

Many advocates of PLCs insist that the use of common assessments is crucial to focusing teacher purpose on student learning. However, these advocates often gloss over the development of these essential tools. We summarize several steps for the development of common assessments. The steps are explained in detail in *Classroom Assessment for Student Learning* (Stiggins et al., 2006) and *Understanding by Design* (Wiggins & McTighe, 2005). We recommend using each of these texts to support the development of common assessments.

The following are our recommended steps for the development of common assessments:

- ◆ Select the most important state or national standards for the grade level and content area. Choose approximately 8 to 10 standards.

- ◆ Deconstruct each standard to determine what students must know and be able to do. Identify the essential knowledge, skills, reasoning, performances, and dispositions that are indicated by the standard. Turn each of these objectives into learning targets.

- ◆ Determine how the learning targets can best be assessed. Different types of assessments are better suited for different types of targets. The best assessment might be a selected response test, a written response, a performance, or a personal communication. The common assessment will use the form of assessment that best matches the greatest number of targets for the standard.

- ◆ Once the best form of assessment is selected, develop a well-constructed assessment using the principles and practices suggested in *Classroom Assessment for Student Learning* (Stiggins et al., 2006).

- ◆ Collect student work samples and use any number of student work protocols to analyze the learning that is evident or missing. Determine if changes in the instruction or assessment are needed to improve student learning.

This process will increase the clarity of classroom level student achievement data; however, an exclusive focus on common assessment data will not assure student success. Failure to include demographic, perception, and school process data will severely limit data-driven decision making. For instance, a common assessment might indicate the students in seventh grade pre-algebra are performing very well. However, the student and parent perception data might reveal that the students are bored with the simplistic math they are performing, and school-process data might reveal that there is no means to identify students who are ready for higher levels of math. Worse yet, the demographic data might reveal that students in poverty are performing at much lower levels on the common assessments. A total profile that includes demographic, perception, achievement, and school processes is needed to focus on specific changes that will improve student learning. We suggest the use of *Using Data to Improve Student Learning* by Victoria Bernhardt (2005) to learn how to create and use these complete data profiles.

Innovation Map One—Student Learning and Growth

The first innovation map (Figure 3.1) naturally focuses our attention on student learning. Take a moment to assess the level of implementation your school has demonstrated. What evidence do you have that your teachers are at this level? What evidence do you have that you, as the leader, are performing at this level? What evidence would you need to move to the next level? How might the answers to the guiding questions change from level to level and help teachers and leaders perceive a need for more or better student achievement data? When we have worked with school districts, the following examples of evidence were suggested for the three levels: student work, student test results, survey results, data profile, and teacher and/or group reflections data profile. What other types of evidence might you have or need in your school or district that demonstrates the levels of implementation for the student learning maps?

Figure 3.1. Innovation Map One—Student Learning and Growth

Guiding questions for increasing implementation levels:
What permits or promotes learning for students? What inhibits or blocks learning for students?

- What is the role of the student in learning?
- How is content organized for effective student learning?
- How are knowledge, reasoning, skill, and dispositions best acquired?
- How is learning best assessed?

Student Learning and Growth

Student Learning/ Growth	Level 1 Implementation		Level 2 Implementation		Level 3 Implementation	
Categories	Teacher	Leader	Teacher	Leader	Teacher	Leader
Goals Develops and commits to student goals for academic, social, and emotional growth.	Sets goals using some general data, mostly regarding student achievement.	Provides general data for goal setting, mostly regarding student achievement.	Sets goals using data that includes achievement, demographics, perceptions, and school processes.	Facilitates collection and analysis of data for achievement, demographics, perceptions, and school processes to develop common goals.	Sets goals using data that has been disaggregated to identify the needs of individual student populations.	Facilitates analysis of data to refine goals to meet the needs of individual student populations.
Outcomes Defines specific outcomes for goals. Monitors and coaches alignment of outcomes to goals.	Aligns some outcomes to achievement data.	Supports development of outcomes aligned to goals and monitors student achievement data.	Analyzes patterns of student needs to identify outcomes aligned to school goals.	Supports alignment of individual and PLC group outcomes to school goals.	Develops outcomes for student groups and individual students to meet goals for each student.	Supports development of outcomes to meet the needs of student groups and individual students.

Figure 3.1. Innovation Map One (continued)

Student Learning/Growth	Level 1 Implementation		Level 2 Implementation		Level 3 Implementation	
Categories	Teacher	Leader	Teacher	Leader	Teacher	Leader
Assessments Establishes common formative and summative assessments.	Uses large-scale tests for summative information. Develops individual formative assessments as part or classroom practice.	Provides large-scale test information. Supports use of formative assessments by individual teachers.	Develops and implements common summative and formative assessments.	Supports development of common formative and summative assessments and monitors and coaches improvements in assessment practices.	Uses differentiated formative assessments to help each student achieve measurable outcomes.	Monitors common assessments for student success.
Practices Changes practices to assure students reach defined goals and standards.	Is aware of best practices yet significant changes have not begun.	Guides development of teacher awareness to best practices that are aligned to defined goals and standards.	Monitors best practices and implements general classroom changes.	Supports improved practices for teaching and learning. Monitors and coaches changes in practices at the classroom level that align with defined goals and standards.	Regularly monitors and changes best practices to meet individual student needs.	Regularly coaches for improvements in teaching, learning, and assessment practices to meet individual student needs.

How Can We Determine If Professional Growth Is Improving Student Learning?

It is unlikely that schools can develop into PLCs without commitment from teachers and leaders. Professional learning communities provide a structure and a process for professionals to learn from each other in a nonthreatening manner and in an environment focused on a collective purpose—improved student learning. This collective purpose does not mean that the sole beneficiaries are students. We must also proclaim professional learning and growth as a visible, desired result of PLCs.

Teaching and learning prosper when they are structured around what we know about how people (teachers as well as students) learn and grow. Research has identified the connection between teacher effectiveness and student learning. The quality of professional growth, in turn, affects the quality of teaching. According to the National Commission on Teaching and America's Future (NCTAF), "Reforms…are rendered effective or ineffective by the knowledge, skills, and commitments of those in schools. Without know-how and buy-in, innovations do not succeed" (1997, p. 7). The NCTAF also contend, "Teacher expertise—what teachers know and can do—affects all core tasks of teaching…No other intervention can make the difference that a knowledgeable, skillful teacher can make in the learning process" (p. 8). Professional growth is essential for improving student learning.

Innovation Map Two—Professional Learning and Growth

We developed a second innovation map (Figure 3.2) to focus attention on professional learning and growth. If we only focus on student learning and growth, the problem for learning will remain with the students. If we have a parallel focus on teacher learning and growth we will assure that we intentionally connect teacher learning and behavior to student learning and achievement. The innovation map parallels the student learning map in guiding questions, components, and levels. Again, we invite you to take a moment to assess the level of implementation your school has demonstrated. What evidence do you have that your teachers are at this level? What evidence do you have that you, as the leader, are performing at this level? What evidence would you need to move to the next level? How might the answers to the guiding questions change from level to level and help teachers and leaders perceive a need for more or better teacher learning data? When we have worked with school districts the following examples of evidence were suggested for the three levels: teacher efficacy instruments; teacher portfolios; teacher/group reflections; documented changes in instruction, curriculum and assessment; and staff development plans. What other types of evidence might you have or need in your school or district that demonstrates the levels of implementation for the teacher learning and growth map?

Figure 3.2. Innovation Map Two—Professional Learning and Growth

Guiding questions for increasing implementation levels:

- What permits or promotes learning for teachers and leaders?
- What inhibits or blocks learning for teachers and leaders?
- What is the role of the teacher and leader in learning?
- How is professional growth organized for effective teacher and leader learning?
- How are knowledge, reasoning, skill, and dispositions best acquired by teachers and leaders?
- How is teacher and leader learning best assessed?
- How is expertise and professional competence developed?

Professional Learning and Growth

Student Learning/ Growth	Level 1 Implementation		Level 2 Implementation		Level 3 Implementation	
Categories	Teacher	Leader	Teacher	Leader	Teacher	Leader
Goals Develops and commits to collective goals for professional development related to teacher/leader academic, social, and emotional growth.	Is aware of professional standards with which to set professional growth goals.	Facilitates the identification of professional standards to set professional growth goals.	Uses professional standards to assess the general level of proficiency of teachers and set goals for professional growth for the school.	Uses professional standards to assess the overall level of proficiency of teachers and facilitates analysis of needs to set goals for professional growth for the school as a whole.	Uses professional standards to assess individual proficiency and to set individual and PLC goals.	Monitors assessment of individual proficiency against professional standards and monitors individual and PLC goals.

Figure 3.2. Innovation Map Two: (continued)

Professional Learning/ Growth Categories	Level 1 Implementation		Level 2 Implementation		Level 3 Implementation	
	Teacher	Leader	Teacher	Leader	Teacher	Leader
Outcomes Aligns individual and group outcomes to professional standards and responsibilities.	Aligns professional development outcomes to professional standards.	Supports alignment of professional development outcomes to professional standards.	Aligns professional development outcomes to school goals.	Supports the development of professional growth outcomes aligned to school goals.	Aligns individual and PLC outcomes to assigned responsibilities in support of school goals.	Supports individual and PLC outcomes aligned to assigned responsibilities in support of school goals.
Assessments Establishes common formative and summative assessments for teacher/leader growth.	Individually determines how to collect and document professional growth.	Permits individuals to determine how to collect and document their growth.	Develops common summative assessments to document professional growth on outcomes.	Supports development of common summative assessments to document professional growth on outcomes.	Develops common formative and summative assessments to document individual and PLC growth.	Supports development of common formative and summative assessments and monitors documentation of individual and PLC growth.
Practices Changes, monitors and coaches professional growth practices to assure growth toward student goals and professional standards.	Develops awareness of best practices for professional growth.	Develops awareness of best practices for professional growth. Promotes application of some practices by faculty.	Implements and monitors best practices for individual and PLC professional growth.	Supports implementation and monitoring of best practices for individual and PLC professional growth.	Consistently monitors impact of instruction on student learning and changes professional practices to meet individual and PLC needs.	Consistently monitors impact of instruction on student learning and supports changes in professional practices to meet individual and PLC needs.

How Do We Know What Needs to Change to Improve Student Learning and Teacher Learning?

Killion's (2002) back-mapping model recommends a cycle of professional development that translates student achievement needs into identified teacher learning needs. These teacher needs are used to identify and implement new learning for teachers in best practices. The cycle concludes with teachers collecting, analyzing, and reflecting on new student achievement data to assess the impact of new learning on students. Foord (2004) used a similar cycle, the change cycle, introduced in Chapter 2 to produce change in a PLC while honoring adult learners. We can gain an understanding of what changes in teaching and learning need to occur by putting into practice the process of moving through a model of change such as the change cycle.

McLaughlin and Talbert (2006) contend that PLCs within schools serve interrelated functions that contribute uniquely to teachers' knowledge base, professionalism, and ability to act on what they learn. Three such functions stand out: teachers build and manage knowledge; teachers create shared language and standards for practice and student outcomes; and teachers sustain aspects of their school's culture vital to continued, consistent norms and instructional practice. From our observations, the second function of shared language and standards for practice is largely absent as is the third. Through the use of Innovation Map One—Student Learning and Growth (see Figure 3.1) and Innovation Map Two—Professional Learning and Growth (see Figure 3.2), school leaders can be attentive to all three functions.

Post Vignette

At the beginning of the chapter, you had a chance to hear a bit about Teresa's challenges as the school leader of her building with the implementation of PLCs. Throughout the chapter information has been shared about the importance (a) of clarifying the purpose of a PLC, (b) of assessing student learning, (c) of assessing teacher and leader learning, and (d) of determining what changes are needed based on student and teacher needs. Now is your chance to practice with the two innovation maps introduced in the chapter. Analyze the following vignette and determine (a) the level of implementation for the teachers, (b) the level of implementation for the leader (Teresa), and (c) the next steps needed for the teachers and the leader to move forward in the implementation of their PLCs.

The school year had begun well. Now in the second year of implementing PLCs, Teresa's teachers seemed appreciative of the opportunity to work together. They were less defensive when asked to complete tasks; they were more agreeable to making changes that impacted student learning, and they were more open to sharing ideas and supporting each other's work. Teresa's use of the student learning and growth map (Innovation Map One) and the professional learning and growth map (Innovation Map Two) of the PLC Implementation Plan had helped her and the teachers in her building analyze their level of implementation and to develop a plan for moving to the next level.

As the school leader Teresa had provided the teachers with student state test results and student demographic information. She had also created a one page overview of the implementation plan from the analysis of Innovation Map One and Innovation Map Two. And, she continued to post articles and other documents in the teacher's lounge that supported the school's professional development topics.

The teachers were using their PLC time to analyze state test results to determine what goals they would set for the school year and to analyze the state standards to decide what changes in curriculum needed to occur. And based on Teresa's demonstrated support for fostering teacher growth, the teachers were discussing the possibility of identifying a select few to attend a national teaching conference in the spring. The tasks completed at each PLC session were recorded on the form developed by the district and modified at the building level, and completed forms were turned in to the principal's office.

Teresa tried to check in with each PLC group on a regular basis and to review the completed PLC forms. One challenge she was encountering was the habit teachers had of reverting to past experiences to address an issue or to come up with a solution concerning a challenge they were facing in their classrooms rather than using recent professional development training, available resources, or current best practices information. The school had invested heavily in professional development that provided them with research-based instructional strategies, curriculum standards and processes, and assessment tools; yet those seemed to be easily forgotten as teachers delved into the day-to-day challenges of teaching. She was unsure about how to replace the pattern with a commitment to using new, research-based practices that would address student needs.

Vignette Analysis

Teresa understands the importance of honoring teacher ownership within the PLCs and the importance of teacher growth in connection with increased student growth. The challenge for her is to establish that sense of respect for teacher knowledge and skill while also heightening the expectation of using identified best practices and assessments. Teresa also needs to increase her focus on assessing the structure and nature of the PLCs—ensuring that the time and process within the PLCs is focused on a clear, common purpose.

Based on the available information, we would contend that Teresa and her teachers are between level 1 and 2 with student learning and growth. We would place them at level 1 with professional growth.

The next steps for Teresa that focus on student learning and growth include providing her teachers with more specific data, tools, and training that focus on assessing the needs of individual student populations. She needs to encourage and support the development of common and summative assessments; and in connection with the development of assessments, she needs to encourage them to monitor the implementation of best practices for teaching and learning. Teresa's leadership team can play a crucial role with communicating and monitoring the use of student assessments.

The next steps that focus on professional growth include the identification and use of professional standards to set professional growth goals that focus on the needs of students. The goals should support the implementation of changes in professional practices and instruction to impact student learning. We would recommend Teresa collaborate with her principal PLC colleagues during the development and implementation of professional growth goals.

Reflecting Forward

Use the following guiding questions for increasing implementation levels for the map(s) associated with this chapter to explore beliefs, assumptions, practices, and evidence that can help you move forward.

- ♦ At what level of implementation are teachers and leaders?
- ♦ What evidence do you have that documents this level of implementation for teachers and leaders?
- ♦ What evidence would you need to move to the next level of implementation?
- ♦ What new learning and resources would you need to move to the next level of implementation?
- ♦ What practices would you need to implement to move to the next level of implementation?
- ♦ What evidence would you collect and reflect on to assess progress to the next level of implementation?
- ♦ Who will you involve when reflecting on your new learning?
- ♦ With whom will you collaborate to improve the learning or implement the new learning across your school/district?

You may find the following form (Figure 3.3) helpful as you process the guiding questions:

Figure 3.3. Guiding Questions Process Form

Where are we, and what evidence do we have of our current level of implementation?	Where do we want to be, and what evidence do we need to move to the next level of implementation?

4

Shared Commitment and Purpose

Vignette 4

Teresa reread her school's mission statement again. Her focus on the mission resulted from an uncomfortable conversation during her principal PLC. She had been feeling pretty good about how PLCs were progressing within her building and she had boldly stated her feelings. However, when her two colleagues pressed her for "proof," Teresa could not produce the evidence. Teresa recalled the strong proclamations made by everyone to actively "live" the mission once the final statement was completed. Now, two years later, there was limited evidence of the school "living" the mission. Was the time spent developing a mission a waste of time? According to PLC experts, a mission answers the question "Why do we exist?" Teresa recalled how diligently they had referred to the mission during their conversations about implementing PLCs. How was the connection lost? Teresa decided she would discuss with her leadership team the value of revisiting the purpose of their mission and of PLCs.

Guiding Questions

- ◆ How can we use PLCs to guide the internalization of purpose and commitment?
- ◆ How do we structure PLCs to encourage and support increased interdependence?

How Can We Use Professional Learning Communities to Guide the Internalization of Purpose and Commitment?

As school leaders we need to provide the culture and the structure for teachers to discuss and reflect on the importance and the value of their involvement in PLCs. Creating the structure and identifying common meeting time is not enough. Sharing the research and documentation is not enough. Teachers need to process and determine for themselves the value of PLCs. They need the time to discuss, reflect, and collectively agree on assumptions, beliefs, and values about teaching and learning. Unless a common understanding of purpose and commitment is established and then used for decision-making within PLCs, the effectiveness will be limited.

DuFour et al. (2006) define "simultaneous loose and tight leadership" as "A leadership concept in which leaders encourage autonomy and creativity (loose) within well-defined parameters and priorities that must be honored (tight)" (p. 218). As school leaders we need to do more than expect that teachers are teaching in a manner in which all students will learn (loose), we need to engage teachers in a collaborative process to study, to clarify, and to commit to teaching in a manner that results in all students learning (tight). A number of structural recommendations have been identified in the research to get at the loose–tight leadership concept; however, the more challenging component is to establish and maintain the relational aspect of the concept. For instance, schools across the nation have identified times in which teachers are instructed to meet in PLC groups—groups that often are determined by the administration. Teachers are directed to focus on a topic or issue; they may be provided with information and/or data to process, and they are asked to derive a strategy or solution that will "improve student learning." Often teachers are being asked to complete and submit a formal form that serves as a report of how their time was used and what decisions were made that will affect student learning.

Rarely is there a request for information concerning their professional growth and needs, much less time allocated to address their needs. The general assumption is that they have been provided an environment that allows them to make some decisions about student learning by meeting as a group (loose) while holding them accountable

> A number of structural recommendations have been identified in the research to get at the loose/tight leadership concept; however, the more challenging component is to establish and maintain the relational aspect of the concept.

as professionals through the reporting process (tight). There appears to be minimal attention paid to establishing buy-in on the purpose or on the level of commitment for the process. Yet without attention to the internalization of purpose and commitment, real institutionalization of the concept of PLCs and the ability to use them as a professional growth process will be minimal. As school leaders we need to attend to both the structural and the relational components of implementation. This can occur by developing a collective understanding and commitment to the purpose of PLCs.

When we have participated in professional development opportunities, we have appreciated facilitators who asked us what we hoped to get out of the experience as well as those who helped us understand how much we already knew or did not know before we began new learning. In one PLC, participants were asked to tell a story about their most effective teaching experience and then, in small teams, construct a sculpture to represent effective education which was shared with the larger group. These brief activities focused attention on the participants' purpose and commitment to effective teaching and began to create a common understanding and language across the entire group.

In their research on reculturing schools, McLaughlin and Talbert (2006) define three professional community types: (a) typical (weak) community, (b) strong traditional community, and (c) learning community. The type of professional community is determined by varying beliefs about technical cultures, professional norms, and organizational policies.

As school leaders we can use McLaughlin and Talbert's defined professional learning types to guide the internalization of purpose and commitment by our staff. McLaughlin and Talbert contend that through coaching and reflection questions we can increase the capacity to change a weak community to a learning community. We agree. Through reflective questioning we can determine the level of community development and commitment within existing PLCs, and we can foster changes in their practices and beliefs that guide them to increased teacher growth, increased student learning, and a stronger commitment to the purpose of PLCs.

Questions must coach for collective capacity and relational responsibility. We must move from questions about individual teacher competence to questions about collective community capacity for competence. The questions should be framed as open possibilities as is done in creative problem solving. In creative problem solving (Treffinger, Isaksen, & Dorval, 2000) the phrase "In what ways might we ..." is used to encourage thinking about many possible solutions from the perspective of group accountability rather than from the efforts of a collection of individuals. By removing the word "I" and inserting the word "We," we can support teachers in developing collective efficacy and commitment as well as a shared, common purpose, as we collaboratively work to increase student achievement.

Using the categories developed by McLaughlin and Talbert (2006), we devised the following reflection or coaching questions (Figure 4.1) to assist in assessing and promoting the development of stronger learning communities.

Figure 4.1. Questions for
Fostering Community Changes in Practices and Beliefs

Professional Community Category	Reflection and/or Coaching Questions to Surface the Level of Community Development and to Foster Changes in Practices and Beliefs in Community
Technical Culture	
Beliefs about students	What permits or promotes learning for students? What inhibits or blocks learning for students?
Student role as learner	What is the role of the student in learning?
Content	How is content organized for effective student learning?
Pedagogy	How are knowledge, skills, and dispositions best acquired?
Assessment practices	How is learning best assessed?
Professional Norms	
Collegial relationships	How are our activities related?
Professional expertise	How do we develop expertise?
Organizational Practices	
Teacher course and/or class assignment	How do we organize ourselves for teaching?
Resource allocation	How do we acquire, distribute, and use resources?

After reflecting on the questions, one school made changes in their daily schedule and in the use of their literacy coach to more effectively implement research-based literacy strategies. The teachers had received training in the strategies and had been individually trying to use them in their classrooms, but they had not had the opportunity to collectively determine what needed to occur building-wide for effective implementation. Not until they were guided through the reflection questions were they able to more clearly understand the magnitude of what they could accomplish as a whole with a more clearly articulated common purpose.

The use of reflection and coaching questions is one way to increase the internalization of purpose and commitment. However, more than questioning needs to occur. Changes in school-wide practices can also increase teachers' commitment to the purpose of PLCs. We again use McLaughlin and Talbert's categories to share examples of change in practices that we have observed that support a commitment to PLCs. What might be examples of changes in practices (Figure 4.2) that occurred within your setting because of the implementation of PLCs?

Figure 4.2. Examples of Changes in Professional Community Practices

Professional Community Category	Learning Community Defined	Examples of Changes in Practices
Technical Culture		
Beliefs about students	All students can achieve at high academic standards.	PLCs are guided through a collective examination of student success and a collective brainstorming of best practice strategies to use with students who have not yet met with success. The school identifies specific practices to implement, monitor, and assess.
Student role as learner	Active role in content learning for all students.	The school establishes as an expectation the implementation of problem-solving strategies and one-on-one teacher-student conversations about learning styles.
Content	Core discipline-based concepts spiraled through curricula.	The school adopts and provides professional development in the implementation of spiraled curricula.
Pedagogy	Bridging subject and student knowledge; learning community.	Teachers in all subject areas match effective teaching strategies with content standards and student knowledge assessments.
Assessment practices	Performance assessments using standards-based rubrics; feedback for improvement.	Teachers develop and implement performance assessments using standard-based rubrics. Student results are collectively assessed.
Professional Norms		
Collegial relationships	Collaboration around teaching and learning; mentoring.	PLCs consistently implement, monitor, and evaluate the internal effectiveness of their group (interpersonal skills, group processing skills, etc.) and the external effectiveness (changes in teaching practices and student assessments).

Professional expertise	Expertise as collective group, based in knowledge shared and developed through collaboration.	The school consistently identifies, reviews, and plans for the exchange of collective expertise developed.
Organizational Practices		
Teacher course or class assignment	Course rotation and sharing for equity and learning.	The use of a literacy specialist to team with teachers to work on implementing specific teaching strategies with students.
Resource allocation	Collective definition of resource needs and sources; resource creation and sharing.	Use of floating substitute teachers to provide PLC groups more time to observe and reflect on each others' practices.

The use of questions and changes in practice are two strategies that encourage the internalization of purpose and commitment. There are a number of other strategies that provide teachers with the opportunity to discuss and internalize the value of PLCs. The specific strategy is not as important as adapting it to meet the needs of your teachers and the culture of your school. It is also important to keep in mind the purpose. Being intentional about why and when teachers process concepts is just as important as being intentional about why and when students process concepts. Often more attention is given to the strategy than to the purpose and the intended outcome.

Making connections, building understanding, and obtaining buy-in are continuous and constant needs with PLCs. With that said, we would like to share activities that we have used as we worked with groups to build purpose and commitment. You will want to reflect on whether or not they will work in your setting; and if so, how they can most effectively be used.

Supporting Professional Learning Center Commitment—Establishing and Honoring Norms

Because of the limited experiences and opportunities to work together, we need to assist teachers with developing a relational commitment to their PLC group. The commitment can begin by asking them to establish and then honor a set of agreed on norms for work and for behavior. Following is a norm sampler sheet (Figure 4.3) that we have used as a means of encouraging groups to have an open discussion about what is important behavior for their group and about how they are going to use the norms to accomplish their work. Addressing norms is not a one-time event. To institutionalize the use of norms, groups need to revisit and reflect on their effectiveness with honoring their established norms.

Figure 4.3. Norm Sampler

Which of the following norms might apply to your learning community? Feel free to add norms as appropriate.

What rules will govern attendance?

- ☐ All members will arrive on time and stay for the entire time.
- ☐ We will start on time and end on time.

What rules will govern how we talk with each other?

- ☐ No zingers or putdowns.
- ☐ All members will join in the team's discussions.
- ☐ Each member will listen attentively as others speak.
- ☐ No one will dominate the discussions.
- ☐ Everyone's point of view will be considered.
- ☐ Our conversations will reflect our respect for and acceptance of one another.
- ☐ We will disagree with ideas, not individuals.
- ☐ We will keep confidential any information shared in confidence.

What other expectations do we have for learning community members?

- ☐ Each team member will commit to participate actively.
- ☐ We will commit to learning with and from each other.
- ☐ We will rotate the team leader role.
- ☐ All members will be prepared for the meeting when they arrive.
- ☐ All members will be totally present during the meeting and will refrain from working on or discussing other things.
- ☐ All members will turn off cell phones or at least put them on vibrate.
- ☐ All members will work to keep team meetings positive and productive.
- ☐ The atmosphere will remain cordial and friendly throughout the meeting.
- ☐ We will have fun and enjoy working together.

What decision-making procedures will be used?

- ☐ We will reach decisions by consensus or agree on a process for making decisions.
- ☐ We will not block action on a decision.

How will we assess our learning community functioning?

- ☐ We will revisit our norms periodically and decide which ones we need to follow better and which ones we need to change.

Building Community—Coat of Arms

One means of providing PLC groups with a process to discuss and establish a common commitment to the purpose of their group is to guide them through the creation of their own Coat of Arms (Figure 4.4). The purpose of the activity is for each small group to create a coat of arms that reflects their collective assumptions, beliefs, and values about the following questions: What are your beliefs about students; what is your role as a learner; what is learning; and what is the meaning of the word "professional"? Groups represent their beliefs with symbols and/or words. Each group also creates a name for their PLC. The activity allows the group to share individual perspectives on the questions and then identify and agree on answers that represent the group. Creating a name for their group supports the concept that they are a collaborative group working together rather than a group of individuals who are grouped together to completed "assigned" tasks. The following are samples of actual coats of arms completed by small PLC groups.

Figure 4.4. Samples of Coat of Arms

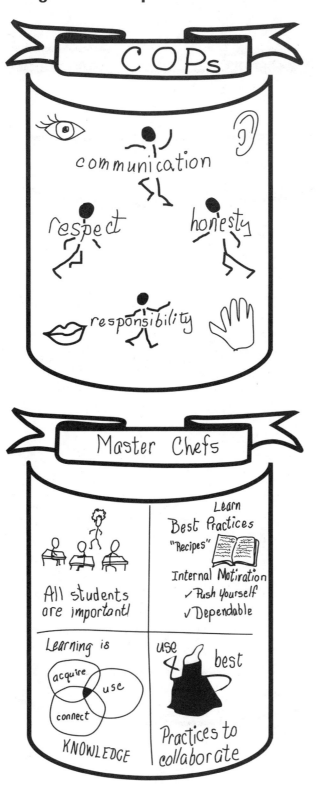

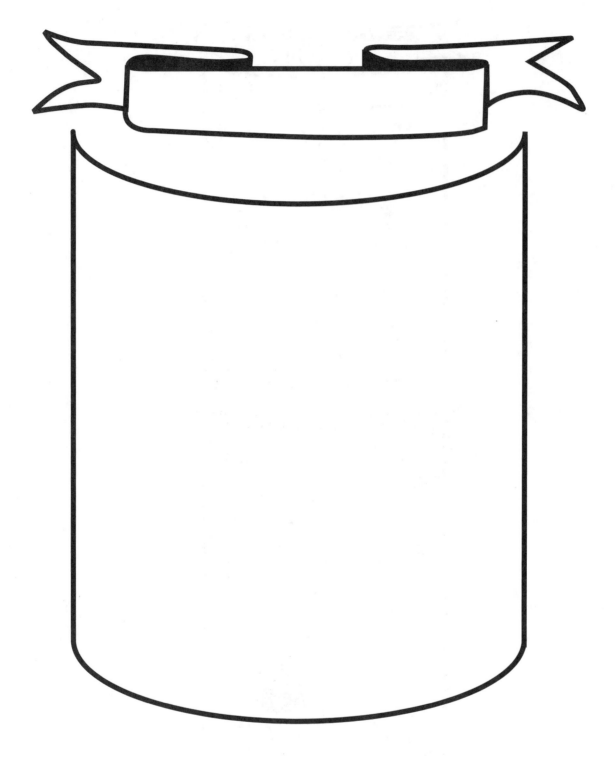

Building Community—Contextual Scan

Another means of establishing a common commitment and understanding of purpose with PLC groups is to have them complete a contextual scan of their current environment. The following is a contextual scan form (Figure 4.5) that asks groups to identify their initial understanding about student achievement, teacher development needs, teacher beliefs, and existing levels of collegiality. An initial sense of commitment and purpose can be created by having small PLC group discussions about their response to the questions followed by whole faculty discussion. An internalized sense of commitment and purpose can be established by revisiting and refining faculty responses to the questions. One principal created an electronic survey using selected questions from the contextual scan. From the individually completed surveys, she compiled a collective response that was discussed at a whole faculty meeting. In this manner she was able to provide everyone with an individual voice but also build a sense of community through a collectively developed response.

Figure 4.5. Contextual Scan

Students

♦ What do students already know and do well? How do you know?

♦ What do students need to learn? How do you know?

Teachers

♦ What do teachers already know and do well? How do you know?

♦ What do teachers need to learn to help meet student needs? How do you know?

Structures for Professional Learning

♦ What are all the ways in which teachers currently learn?

♦ Which methods are working or not working? How do you know?

Current Initiatives for Changes in Practice

♦ What are all the new teaching initiatives introduced in the last three years?

♦ Which initiatives are working or not working? How do you know?

Beliefs

♦ What do most of the teachers in your school believe about students? How do you know?

♦ What do most of the teachers believe is the role of the student in learning?

♦ What do most of the teachers believe is their role in learning?

♦ What do most of the teachers believe about effective teaching and assessment?

♦ What do most of the teachers believe is professional practice?

Cultural Compatibility

♦ Which teachers seem to work well together? How do you know?

♦ Why do some teachers seem to work well together and some do not?

A common mistake in PLCs is to assume that we identify our purpose and make our commitment at the beginning of the year and are finished. Leaders must monitor purpose and commitment to assure that PLCs are on course or to make course corrections. This contextual scan or selected questions from the contextual scan can be repeated at different times during the year to recommit and redefine purpose.

Building Community—Shared Values

Commitment to the purpose of PLCs can also be increased by establishing a set of shared values. A shared set of values can serve as a means of focus by which groups can identify with as they collaboratively work together. We have used the following process (Figure 4.6) to guide groups through the process of identifying a core set of values.

Figure 4.6. Shared Values

Commitment to a shared mission, vision, and goals requires alignment of our values as well. Do we share the same values in our PLCs?

The following list contains some key words that represent values. Please add your own key words to the list if you don't see them. Read through the whole list to select the five most important values that resonate with your beliefs. List those five values in order of their importance to you in the space below, with one being the most important and five the least important of the five values.

Achievement	Excitement	Insight	Passion	Spontaneity
Adventure	Expression	Integrity	Patriotism	Stability
Authenticity	Family	Justice	Perfection	Status
Awareness	Fashion	Kindness	Playfulness	Subtlety
Beauty	Freedom	Knowledge	Pleasure	Teaching
Charity	Friendship	Leadership	Power	Time
Community	Fun	Learning	Recognition	Tradition
Compassion	Generosity	Loyalty	Religion	Truth
Competition	Growth	Love	Respect	Winning
Creativity	Honesty	Money	Responsibility	Wisdom
Discipline	Humility	Nature	Security	Working
Diversity	Humor	Novelty	Sensitivity	
Ecology	Imagination	Order	Serenity	
Excellence	Independence	Originality	Spirituality	

(Values list taken from Gelb, M. J. (1999). *How to think like Leonardo da Vinci workbook.* New York: Dell.)

My Top Values:

1. _____

2. _____

3. _____

4. _____

5. _____

Compare your five top values with those of your PLC group. How are your values alike; how are they different? How might the differences affect your PLC's commitment to spending one hour per week working together to improve student achievement?

Defining Profession Learning Community Purpose—Analysis of Assumptions and Values

Senge (1995) notes that often times what is "unseen" by groups are mental models, underlying structures, patterns of behavior, and values (Figure 4.7). What is "seen" at the tip of the pyramid are events. During this analysis of assumptions and values activity, groups are asked to use the reflection questions for technical cultures, professional norms, and organizational practices (McLaughlin & Talbert, 2006) to determine what the events at the tip of the pyramid look like. Then, they are asked to move down through the pyramid to uncover patterns of behavior, underlying structures, and mental models and values that produce the events. Professional learning community groups are asked to clarify how changes made that support the purpose and commitment of PLCs in the "unseen" portion of the pyramid can change the visible events at the tip.

Figure 4.7. Pyramid of Purpose

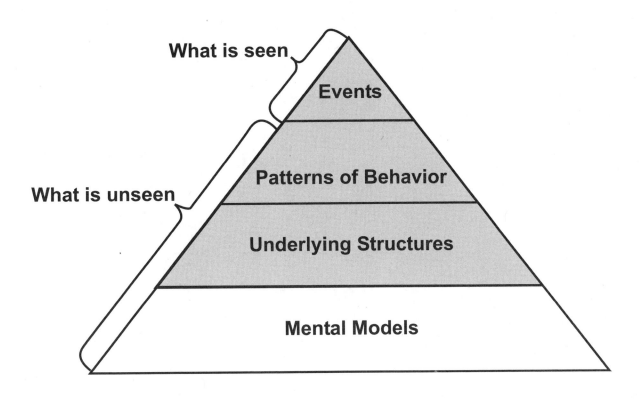

Defining Professional Learning Community Purpose— Ask Why Five Times

Once PLC groups have examined and developed a collective set of assumptions and values, the commitment to the collective set can be strengthened by completing the following "Ask why five times" activity (Figure 4.8). PLCs generally serve four purposes: promote student learning, promote adult learning, professionalize teaching practices, and change education. If values are closely aligned to these purposes, commitment to work in the PLC is enhanced. Groups are guided to ask why about each purpose five successive times to discover their underlying values about (a) why PLCs promote student learning, (b) why PLCs promote teacher learning, (c) why PLCs professionalize practice, and (d) why PLCs change education. Each time you answer the why question, ask why to the answer. The activity helps groups uncover the degree of alignment of their values to the four purposes of PLCs.

Figure 4.8. Defining Professional Learning Community Purpose: Asking Why Five Times

Professional learning communities are generally recommended to achieve four purposes: promote student learning, promote adult learning, professionalize teaching practices, and change education. If values are closely aligned to these purposes, commitment to work in the PLC is enhanced. This activity will help you uncover the degree of alignment of your values to the four key purposes for PLCs.

For each of the key PLC purposes, ask "why?" five successive times to surface your underlying assumptions, beliefs, and values related to that purpose. Each time you answer the why questions, ask why to the answer.

1. Promote student learning

   Why? _____

   Why? _____

   Why? _____

   Why? _____

   Why? _____

   What is your motivation for promoting student learning through the use of PLCs?

2. Promote teacher learning

   Why? _____

   Why? _____

   Why? _____

   Why? _____

   Why? _____

   What is your motivation for promoting teacher learning through the use of PLCs?

3. Professionalize teaching practices

Why? _____

Why? _____

Why? _____

Why? _____

Why? _____

What is your motivation for professionalizing practice through the use of PLCs?

4. Change education

Why? _____

Why? _____

Why? _____

Why? _____

Why? _____

What is your motivation for professionalizing practice through the use of PLCs?

In one school district, a team of principals completed all four of the Ask Why activities and found that they were motivated to create future leaders who would save the world from destruction. They sincerely believed that PLCs were essential to world peace and prosperity. This type of deep commitment to core values or needs often surfaces when PLC groups dig deep to uncover their true purpose.

How Do We Structure Professional Learning Communities to Encourage and Support Increased Interdependence?

There are structural components of PLCs that support the increased internalization of purpose and commitment to the PLC concept. For instance, the size and the makeup of groups send an important message to the value placed on PLCs. If we as leaders are given the opportunity to establish PLCs, we have a responsibility to carefully determine how teachers are grouped. Research supports the optimal group size of a PLC as three-four members per group. Our experiences with schools and PLCs reinforce the research. The size allows for each member of the group to have a voice. The size also minimizes the number of communication transactions to which each member must attend, which increases listening and minimizes the number of miscommunications. With each increase in membership in a PLC, the number of messages and possible concomitant difficulties expands exponentially (Johnson et al., 2006).

Equally as important is the makeup of the group. Careful consideration should be given to who is included and why they are included. This especially needs to be addressed with teachers often times characterized as "specialists" (i.e., literacy specialists, special education teachers, testing coordinators). Depending on the purpose of the PLCs and on the mission of the school, it may be most beneficial for specialists to establish their own PLC or to join other PLC groups. We have observed the effectiveness of both. For instance, one district determined it would be most beneficial for their special education staff to develop and meet within their own PLCs. Their intent was to allow those groups to collectively strengthen their own expertise in their respective areas and then, in turn, share that knowledge with others in the district (i.e., general education teachers, administration, counselors, paraprofessionals). Within the same district, however, literacy specialists join general education teacher PLC groups in an effort to more closely connect literacy-based research best practices with curriculum.

Grouping teachers effectively allows for optimal focus on changes with instruction, curriculum, and assessment. Murphy and Lick (1998) note that the most obvious strength of whole-faculty study groups is the support the groups give each other by providing them with a forum for (a) establishing and working toward shared goals, (b) breaking through barriers among themselves, (c) building individual, team, and organizational resilience, (d) planning and learning more effectively, (e) learning to deal with what is while envisioning what can be, and (f) translating principles of teaching and learning into real practice.

Time plays a crucial role in the effectiveness of PLCs. Teachers are being asked to learn and implement changes in a number of areas (i.e., teaching practices, beliefs, procedures). Ask teachers what is necessary to implement the changes needed to increase student achievement and they will resoundingly tell you "time." As school leaders, we need to assure adequate time to implement changes. However, just as crucial, is our understanding that once teachers are committed to the importance of PLCs, that time should not be completely controlled by administration. When teachers or school leaders think that PLC "changes" only happen on PLC early release days, it is a sign of dependent, technician behavior (McLaughlin & Talbert, 2006). The goal should be for teachers to assume that PLCs are the way they live their whole day. Teachers committed to the purpose will find numerous opportunities to discuss teaching and learning. For instance, we have witnessed teachers who view student passing time as an opportunity to consult on students, strategies, and materials. We have also witnessed teachers whose commitment to professional learning in community became so important that they voluntarily scheduled daily PLC time for the first half hour of every school day. Teachers and leaders will claim time is a structural barrier to PLC change until the value of time spent in PLCs becomes so evident that the time becomes a cultural norm representing professionalism.

As school leaders we can encourage such thinking, and we can ensure that teachers have as many opportunities as possible to collaborate. Murphy and Lick (1998) contend, "Frequency and regularity of meetings are key elements for successful study groups. …Because implementation of innovations is a key function of study groups, proximity is important. Teachers who work in the same building and have common training can more easily work on implementation concerns together" (p. 6). Schmoker (1996) states "When [teachers] began to see collective progress, a direct result from of their focused collaboration, the meetings become more meaningful" (p. 11). He contends, "The nature of the complex work of teaching 'cannot be accomplished by the most knowledgeable individuals working alone'" (Little, 1990, p. 520 cited in Schmoker, 1996, p. 12). Teachers often realize in a short time, they can collectively craft effective coherent lessons and assessments. Many also realize that such careful lesson planning, matched with a carefully built assessment, increases student learning.

Finally, as school leaders we need to ensure resources (human and fiscal) for effective PLC implementation. Given how challenging it has become to secure and protect resources in an era of limited funding, we need to seek new venues and strategies involving resources. Professional development funds no longer (and maybe never did) cover all the needs for teaching and student learning. Schools have realized the importance of internal and external support and collaboration to ensure resources are available. Identifying community expertise and resources, securing external grants, and creatively using internal resources are required of all school personnel as we work to institutionalize PLCs. The positive aspect of this is that we can implement and sustain PLCs in a manner that actually capitalizes on the often underused expertise of teachers and others. Examples of tapping into unused resources are endless; for instance, through our university partnerships, university professors have shared their research and areas of expertise with K–12 partners (i.e., strategies and skills for differentiating instruction and culturally responsive classrooms; analyzing data, and assessing student learning). We have also observed through our own graduate students' work that they are setting goals in their PLCs to use parent and paraprofessional resources more effectively. They have prepared materials and processes and/or systems aligned to best practices so that parents and paraprofessionals (human resources) perform support functions that align with their teaching practices. One principal who worried that her teachers were too dependent on her as the "resident expert" identified teachers with expertise based on her classroom observations and provided them with time and money to develop descriptions of strategies and resources so that they could become the "resident experts" for the following year. In this way, she decreased dependency on her and increased the resources for all of her staff.

Innovation Map Three—
Professional Learning Community Development

We developed a third innovation map (Figure 4.9) to focus attention on PLC development specifically on the components of purpose and commitment. If these two components are not systematically developed and shared, no amount of structural design for PLCs will produce teacher growth and student achievement increases. This map uses different guiding questions to uncover assumptions about purpose and commitment. Please pause to assess the level of implementation your school has demonstrated. What evidence do you have that your teachers are at this level? What evidence do you have that you, as the leader, are performing at this level? What evidence would you need to move to the next level? How might the answers to the guiding questions change from level to level and help teachers and leaders clarify their understanding about purpose and commitment in their PLCs? When we have worked with school districts the following examples of evidence were suggested for the three levels: district and school level policies and procedures, outcomes of staff development plans, outcomes of continuous improvement plans. What other types of evidence might you have or need in your school or district that demonstrates the levels of implementation PLC purpose and commitment?

Figure 4.9. Innovation Map Three—Professional Learning Community Development

Guiding questions for increasing implementation levels:
- What do we agree to hold in common with our colleagues?
- What type of commitments do we make with our colleagues?

PLC Development

PLC Development Categories	Level 1 Implementation		Level 2 Implementation		Level 3 Implementation	
	Teacher	**Leader**	**Teacher**	**Leader**	**Teacher**	**Leader**
Purpose Develops and monitors adherence to purpose, core values, and norms.	Develops common purpose, core values, and norms.	Supports development of common purposes, core values, and norms.	Monitors learning community purpose, core values, and norms on a regular basis and modifies as needed.	Monitors assessment of learning community purposes, core values, and norms on a regular basis and supports modifications.	Plans and implements improvements to sustain common purpose, core values, and norms.	Supports and coaches improvement plans to sustain common purpose, core values, and norms.
Commitment Develops and monitors adherence to academic, physical, and social commitments.	Develops common academic, physical, and social commitments.	Supports development of common academic, physical, and social commitments.	Monitors common academic, physical, and social commitments. Celebrates commitments.	Monitors and coaches assessment of common academic, physical, and social commitments. Celebrates commitments.	Assesses changes in the structure and nature of the community. Celebrates changes and successes from committed actions.	Monitors changes in the structure and nature of the community. Celebrates changes and successes from committed actions.

Post Vignette

At the beginning of the chapter, Teresa's concerns about how to get teachers to internalize purpose and develop commitment were shared. She also contemplated the effectiveness of her school's PLCs. Following Teresa's vignette, we provided you with information and strategies about how to strengthen purpose and commitment and about how to establish effective structures that can lead to sustainable PLCs. Based on the information shared in this chapter and through the use of the PLC Implementation Plan Three—PLC Development, analyze the following vignette and determine (a) the level of implementation involving purpose and commitment for the teachers, (b) the level of implementation involving purpose and commitment for the leader (Teresa), and (c) the next steps needed for the teachers and the leader to move forward in the implementation of their PLCs.

Teresa read through the latest forms submitted by the PLC groups in her building. Each of the groups had diligently completed the forms; however, as Teresa reviewed them she was disheartened. Most seemed to be completed in a manner similar to assignments she collected when she was a teacher where students had simply filled in the answers rather than really delved into learning the content. There were, of course, a few forms (similar again to the classroom assignment) that revealed deep thinking, intentional planning, and identifiable strategies. These were the PLC groups that seemed to grasp the concepts and challenges from the beginning. They were also the groups that had quickly established common goals and commitments within their PLCs. The challenge for Teresa was that she needed her entire staff to function in such a manner.

Determined to establish a school-wide sense of purpose and commitment to PLCs, Teresa met with the school's professional development committee and requested use of the next available professional development time. During the half day session, Teresa guided her staff through the Coat of Arms activity as well as the Ask Why Five Times activity. Her teachers were surprised at the differences that surfaced among them about assumptions, beliefs, and values about teaching and learning. However, because they had already been meeting in PLCs, there was enough trust and collaboration established for them to work through the differences and agree on a set of common purposes and values.

Teresa also had teachers reflect on what was going well with PLCs and what was not going so well. Responses from that activity served as a reminder to Teresa of the need to take time to acknowledge the successes that were occurring because of existing commitments to PLC work. The process also surfaced some concerns about the present structure of some of the groups. Two specific changes were requested: (a) a regrouping of the size of PLCs from sizes of seven to eight members to three to four members, and (b) a regrouping of the makeup of some of the groups—specifically the special education teachers and resource teachers requested being grouped into a PLC themselves rather than being divided up and assigned to various grade level PLCs.

Vignette Analysis

We applaud Teresa's openness to revisiting the internalization of purpose and commitment by her teachers. Given how little is often available for professional development time, it is difficult sometimes to take what could be considered a step back and reexamine what may have been previously addressed. However, if buy-in is missing or if the level of implementation desired is not occurring then it is imperative that a school leader take the time to approach these issues. To plow ahead without reexamining and refining processes and procedures, will threaten the development and sustainability of PLCs

Based on the above vignette we would contend that Teresa and her staff are probably teetering between level 1 and level 2 of implementation on the PLC Implementation Plan Three—PLC Development. It appears that some groups have developed a common purpose, values and norms and have committed to common commitments; however, it also appears as though a number of groups have not. There is limited information also of Teresa's role in monitoring and coaching the groups with assessing their adherence to purpose and commitment.

Next steps for Teresa and her teachers would include following through with requested changes in the size and the makeup of the PLC groups. Having established a set of common purposes and values, the teachers will need to be encouraged and coached on their efforts to adhere to them as they continue to develop and monitor their adherence to the academic, physical, and social commitments they make. Teresa will need to establish a process for herself that allows her the time to adequately attend, monitor, and coach the groups. Teresa should also determine how the individual PLC groups can effectively share their successes and changes with the rest of the groups. The opportunity to share strategies, changes, and successes with the large group allows for those changes to be implemented in a broader manner and it allows for teachers' knowledge, skills and abilities to be recognized and celebrated.

Reflecting Forward

Use the following guiding questions for increasing implementation levels for the map(s) associated with this chapter to explore beliefs, assumptions, practices, and evidence that can help you move forward.

- ◆ At what level of implementation are teachers and leaders?
- ◆ What evidence do you have that documents this level of implementation for teachers and leaders?
- ◆ What evidence would you need to move to the next level of implementation?
- ◆ What new learning and resources would you need to move to the next level of implementation?
- ◆ What practices would you need to implement to move to the next level of implementation?
- ◆ What evidence would you collect and reflect on to assess progress to the next level of implementation?
- ◆ Who will you involve when reflecting on your new learning?
- ◆ With whom will you collaborate to improve the learning or implement the new learning across your school/district?

You may find the following form (Figure 4.10) helpful as you process the guiding questions.

Figure 4.10. Guiding Questions Process Form

Where are we, and what evidence do we have of our current level of implementation?	Where do we want to be, and what evidence do we need to move to the next level of implementation?

5

Effective Interactions

Vignette 5

Teresa was delighted that teams had developed norms and group goals. The formation of PLC structures had proceeded smoothly. However, just when she thought they could move forward as learners, trouble surfaced. A team consisting of her most seasoned teachers was ready to pull the plug. The team leader reported constant interpersonal conflicts, lack of participation by members, unprofessional behavior at meetings, failure to follow-through on agreements, and called them "the team from hell." One member was threatening to file a union grievance because this work was not in their contract. Teresa worried that the negativity would spread to other teams. She noted the contrast in behaviors to her "dream team." This high flying team had a natural chemistry and its members were socially adept and excellent problem solvers. How could she duplicate their capabilities to assure that all teams were effective teams? Principals in her principal PLC faced the same issues and they decided to tackle the problem together by learning about interpersonal skills, conflict management, and interdependent teaming strategies.

Guiding Questions

- Why is relational effectiveness important for PLCs?
- How can we develop cooperative, collaborative PLCs?
- How can we build interdependent relationships in PLCs?
- What strategies can increase interpersonal and group skills in PLCs?
- How can we assure individual and group accountability?

In Chapters 3 and 4 we focused on developing purpose and commitment toward improved student and teacher learning. This chapter focuses on understanding the human and relational factors that affect the development of PLCs. PLC success requires highly functional human interactions. Some leaders will tell you "it's all about relationships," and they are partly right. We have seen leaders who focus only on effective relationships to the detriment of focused, goal-driven results. To execute commonly defined purposes, successful learning communities depend on effective interdependence, interpersonal communication, and group processes, as well as collective responsibility and accountability. These traits are human relations skills and may or may not appear as strengths in our teachers. Despite the fact that most teachers take a course in human relations in teacher preparation programs, the focus has remained on developing relationships with students and their families, not on relationships with teaching colleagues. The long history of privatized practice in education has also limited the need to develop competence in interacting with other teachers. Creating shared understanding through effective communication, group processes, and relational responsibility is not the focus of our professional practice. We won't necessarily hear teachers talking in the lounge about how well their team is building on each other's ideas to reach consensus on their interdependent goals, but we should.

When PLCs fail, it usually is not because the school goals were the wrong goals. It is usually not because the administration failed to provide structures for team work. Failure is usually the result of failed relationships that prevent collaboration for optimal

> Successful learning communities depend on effective interdependence, interpersonal communication, group processes, as well as collective responsibility and accountability.

learning and promote further teacher isolation to escape escalating interpersonal conflicts.

Proponents of PLCs explain that when responsibility is focused on student results, teacher learning will also become focused. They assume that the focus on students will naturally elicit responsibility for positive relationships and learning among teachers. Two faulty assumptions in this thinking lie at the heart of problems with implementation. First, the desire to help students achieve does not translate automatically into responsibility for relationships and learning with other PLC members; it translates into figuring out what the individual teacher needs to do to raise his or her students' achievement. Second, if proper reasons and incentives are incorporated into the implementation of PLCs, teachers will be motivated to assume responsibility for their relationships and mutual learning. This, however, also assumes that teachers naturally possess the social intelligence or competence to execute this responsibility. For learning communities to thrive, professional learning must focus on social competence as well as teaching competence to produce changes in student achievement.

Social competence, according to Daniel Goleman (2007), "can be organized into two broad categories: social awareness, what we sense about others—and social facility, what we then do with that awareness" (p. 84). Each of these broad categories contains a spectrum of competencies. Social awareness includes primal empathy in which we feel with others and sense nonverbal emotions, attunement where we listen with full receptivity, empathic accuracy in understanding another person's thoughts, feelings, and intentions, and social cognition of how the social world works, or the spoken and unspoken rules for building teams, alliances, or friendships. Social facility includes synchrony or smooth interactions at the nonverbal level, self-presentation where our emotional expressions support our verbal message, influence or the ability to shape the outcomes of our interactions, concern for the needs of others and acting accordingly. These categories interact with one another to produce social transactions that can either support or weaken relationships in PLCs. If members listen with full receptivity and in doing so develop deep empathic accuracy, they will be better able to synchronize their interactions, understand the social norms or rules, and use their genuine concern to shape the outcomes of their interactions. If members express hurtful or false judgments in the social interaction, they weaken empathy and concern, violate the social rules, and use negative self-presentation and influence to produce negative outcomes.

To be successful, PLCs must develop social awareness and social facility; both are developed within dialogue. Peter Senge et al. (2000) argues that effective dialogue is an essential discipline that must be practiced in a learning organization.

> Storytelling increases the number of comparisons of new experiences to prior experiences for adults and therefore increases learning and retention.

The goal of dialogue is to open new ground by establishing a "container" or "field" for inquiry: a setting where people can become more aware of the context around their experience, and of the processes of thought and feeling that created the experience. In the practice of dialogue, we pay attention not only to the words but to the spaces between the words; not only to the result of an action but to its timing; not only to the things people say but to the timbre and tones of their voices. . . During the dialogue process, people learn how to think together—not just in the sense of analyzing a shared problem or creating new pieces of shared knowledge but in the sense of occupying a collective sensibility, in which the thoughts, emotions, and resulting actions belong not to one individual, but to all of them together. (p. 75)

This collective sensibility can make the conversation so focused that members lose track of time, finish each others' statements, develop ideas effortlessly, and appear unaware of outside disturbances.

Effective dialogue also supports learning by expanding perspectives through reflection and inquiry. "In any new experience, most people are drawn to take in and remember only the information that reinforces their existing mental model. . . .The core task of the discipline of mental models is bringing tacit assumptions and attitudes to the surface so people can explore and talk about their differences and misunderstandings with minimal defensiveness" (Senge et al., 2000, p. 67). Senge suggests that two skills must be applied within dialogue to address the impact of mental models: reflection to slow down thinking about mental models and inquiry to seek answers to questions not already known.

In effective dialogue, relational responsibility is constructed at the center of the group not as separate interactions among members and transforms the identity of each member in the construction of the relationship (McNamee & Gergen, 1999). Bossidy and Charan (2002) contend, "Dialogue is the core of culture and the basic unit of work. How people talk to each other absolutely determines how well the organization will function. Is the dialogue stilted, politicized, fragmented, and butt-covering? Or is it candid and reality-based, raising the right questions, debating them, and finding realistic solutions?" (p. 25). They also argue that "the leader has to be on the same playing field," consistently practicing and modeling effective dialogue.

Conflict arises in dialogue when there is a "perceived divergence of interest, or a belief that the parties' current aspirations cannot be achieved simultaneously" (Rubin, Pruitt, & Kim, 1994, p. 5). Dialogue to surface identities, interests, norms, past achievements, mental models, and current or future aspirations can prevent or resolve social conflict. Social bonds can be systematically developed and might include: feelings of acceptance; common understandings about beliefs, experiences, and threats; common kinship, language, or culture; dependent and interdependent roles or responsibilities; or common history (Rubin, et al., 1994).

Professional learning communities require effective, collaborative dialogue among teachers and this, in turn, requires systems to support the development of social competence. Fortunately for us, systems to develop cooperative and collaborative learners have been present for the last 40 years.

How Can We Develop Cooperative, Collaborative Professional Learning Communities?

Systems for effective cooperative classrooms were developed by Johnson and Johnson in the 1960s and became standard practices in many elementary classrooms and some secondary classrooms. The principles of cooperative learning were translated into effective practices for adult learners by Johnson et al. (2006) and into practices of collaborative learning by Barkley, Cross, and Major (2005). Guided by their work, we can produce PLCs with effective interdependence, interpersonal communication, group processes, and individual and group accountability. We correlated the conditions in cooperative learning classrooms to those leaders can foster in effective PLCs in Figure 5.1.

Figure 5.1. Cooperative Learning in Professional Learning Communities

Conditions in Effective Cooperative Learning Classrooms	Conditions in Effective Professional Learning Communities
Positive Interdependence ♦ Group goals are clearly defined and understood by all members. ♦ Roles and responsibilities are clearly defined. ♦ It is clear to the members how they must rely on and support the work of others to achieve the goal. ♦ Resources are shared to produce mutually defined results.	PLC and/or School Goal Interdependence ♦ Clear SMART* goals for school and PLC. ♦ It is clear to all members (PLC & school) how they rely on and support each other. ♦ Members make a formal commitment to their roles and responsibilities to meet the PLC and school goal. ♦ The principal and/or superintendent clarify plans, roles, and responsibilities of those not in alignment with the school or district goals. Expectations are clarified for all. ♦ Resources, rewards, and celebrations are aligned to support cooperative interdependence in achieving the goals not to support competition among members. Rewards are for the execution of cooperative interdependence to help all achieve the goal, not comparisons of teacher and/or student scores to see who achieved their own goal. Solidarity toward the group goal raises commitment by all participants.
Face to Face Interaction ♦ Significant interaction time is planned (usually daily) to permit team functioning. ♦ Base groups are long term (usually all year). ♦ Ad hoc groups are for short-term goals. ♦ Members help other members with attendance and goal attainment.	PLC Team Interaction Time ♦ Daily interaction is best; weekly is a minimum. ♦ Team stays together for the year. ♦ Book studies and committees are considered ad hoc teams. ♦ Attendance is essential—nothing takes the precedence of the team meeting.

Conditions in Effective Cooperative Learning Classrooms	Conditions in Effective Professional Learning Communities
	PLC Team Interaction Time (cont) • Structures to permit time include use of common prep, weekly morning meetings, weekly faculty meetings, weekly substitute teachers to release staff for meetings, exploratory replacement curriculum, or events to release teachers.
Interpersonal Skill Development • Developmental skills are listed, defined, taught, and assessed by students and teacher. • Definitions are articulated for each skill and are systematically monitored for successful use. Observable behaviors define what the skill looks like and sounds like in action. • Achievement of these skills is as important as content achievement and is monitored and celebrated.	Interpersonal Skills for PLCs • Norms and interpersonal skills are listed, defined, taught (when needed), and assessed by teachers in their PLC and by principals. • Skills such as listening, paraphrasing, encouraging, or clarifying must be effectively used by teachers. PLC success requires high functioning group dynamics and relational responsibility. • Norms and interpersonal skills are systematically monitored for successful use. Successes are recognized as contributions to the positive culture and morale of the team and school. • Achievement of these skills is as important as new teaching skills or student achievement.
Group Processing • Roles and responsibilities are defined, assigned, and rotated. • The group processes their work by monitoring and reflecting on both achievement and interpersonal goals. • Processing of the group interactions takes place at the end of each session. • The group uses processing information to discuss, draft, and implement changes in the way the group works.	PLC Processing • The group develops and follows a meeting protocol to assure effective use of time. • Roles and responsibilities are defined, assigned, and rotated. • Skills for making decisions, solving problems, setting goals, and executing plans are learned by all members.

Conditions in Effective Cooperative Learning Classrooms	Conditions in Effective Professional Learning Communities
	PLC Processing (cont) ♦ The group processes their work by monitoring and reflecting on both achievement and interpersonal goals. A principal or professional development coordinator can help groups select interpersonal and group-processing goals and provide supporting instruction at faculty meetings. ♦ The meeting protocol itself requires processing and planning for improvement of the group's skills. ♦ Documenting reflection on group processes is a way to assure that the group attends to their norms and to the growth of not only the group but each individual. As the culture changes or members change, this action is crucial for effective learning in the PLC. Inattention to changes can physically, psychologically, intellectually, and emotionally derail the group.
Independent and Group Accountability ♦ A group product is developed with individual parts contributing to the final product. ♦ Individuals share their products and use them to formulate an improved group product and also to revise their individual work.	Independent and Group Accountability ♦ Individuals account for their personal goals, learning, efforts, roles, and/or responsibilities toward the group goal. ♦ Groups account for the alignment of their group goals, learning, efforts, roles, and/or responsibilities toward the school goal. ♦ Individual portfolios contribute to individual evaluations by principals and include personal and peer coaching assessments aligned to professional standards, professional learning, interpersonal achievement in the group, reflections, and plans for the future.

Conditions in Effective Cooperative Learning Classrooms	Conditions in Effective Professional Learning Communities
	Independent and Group Accountability (cont)
	◆ Group portfolios contain contributions to the interdependent goals of the group and include meeting protocols, group processing forms or discussions, group learning, group interpersonal and processing achievements, group reflections, and group plans for the future.
	◆ Performance is compared to expectations set and plans for future action are developed between the principal and each individual and PLC group.
	◆ Assessment for learning (Stiggins, 2005) practices are employed with teachers and PLCs. Clear targets, effective multiple assessments, timely and specific feedback in the form of coaching questions permits self-assessment and motivation to improve.

The next sections explain strategies for developing interdependence, interpersonal communication, group processing, and accountability in support of cooperative, collaborative cultures in PLCs.

How Can We Build Interdependent Relationships and Goals in Professional Learning Communities?

Interdependence is created when members of a PLC develop shared understanding about their roles, responsibilities, and goals. Positive interdependence is characterized by group goals, group celebrations, division of labor, shared resources, and assigned roles and responsibilities. Members also commit to processes for continuous improvement to work interdependently toward shared results.

We developed a fourth innovation map (Figure 5.2) to focus on the development of interdependent goals, responsibilities and continuous improvement in PLCs. This innovation map parallels the previous maps with guiding questions, components, and levels of implementation.

Figure 5.2. Innovation Map Four—Interdependence

Guiding questions for increasing implementation levels:

- How are our activities related?
- How do we acquire, distribute, and use resources?
- How do we go about deciding when to seek assistance or coordinate learning activities with other colleagues?
- How do we plan for improvements in student learning and professional growth with colleagues?

Interdependence

Interdependence Categories	Level 1 Implementation		Level 2 Implementation		Level 3 Implementation	
	Teacher	Leader	Teacher	Leader	Teacher	Leader
Relational goals and responsibilities Develops relational goals and responsibilities.	Develops awareness of ways in which teachers might share resources, roles, and responsibilities.	Develops awareness of the ways in which PLCS can share resources, roles, and responsibilities.	Develops interdependent PLC goals with shared resources, roles, and responsibilities clearly defined.	Monitors PLC goals for inter-dependence and coaches for clarity of shared resources, roles, and responsibilities.	Consistently sets and assesses interdependent goals for shared resources, roles, and responsibilities.	Monitors and coaches for consistent use of interdependent goals, with shared resources, roles and responsibilities.
Continuous improvement cycle Adheres to a continuous improvement cycle.	Commits to development of interdependent goals and the use of a continuous improvement process.	Facilitates development of commitment to interdependent goals and the use of a continuous improvement process.	Implements process to understand, internalize, operationalize, and evaluate changes in student achievement and professional growth.	Facilitates implementation of process to understand, internalize, operationalize, and evaluate changes in student achievement and professional growth.	Consistently uses continuous improvement process to analyze and make improvements in student achievement and professional growth.	Assesses the consistent use of the continuous improvement process. Coaches improvements in the application of the process.

Again, we invite you to take a moment to assess the level of implementation in your school. What evidence do you have that your teachers are at this level? What evidence do you have that you, as the leader, are performing at this level? What evidence would you need to move to the next level? How might the answers to the guiding questions change from level to level and help teachers and leaders develop greater interdependence? What other types of evidence might you have or need in your school or district that demonstrates the levels of implementation for the interdependence map?

To increase interdependence, PLCs can explore issues of interdependence using the following questions (Figure 5.3). Leaders can encourage PLCs to share ideas about interdependence with other PLCs during faculty meetings to accelerate the development of less experienced groups.

Figure 5.3. Reflective Questions to Develop Interdependence

- What are the norms or values and traditions for the ways people treat each other?
- Who leads? How do members conceive of their roles, rights, and responsibilities?
- What actions and resources will support learning? What will get in the way of learning?
- How should members behave toward each other to support individual and group learning?
- What kinds of things should we agree we won't do in the community or outside the community?
- How often should we review our learning agreement?
- Who do we want to join us?
- When and where will we meet?
- How will we record the conditions of our learning community?
- What will we do to reinforce our learning agreement or if our agreement is broken?
- What agreements need to the made about membership, keeping on schedule, bringing refreshments, and making decisions?
- What rituals or ceremonies are important to our community?
- How will we monitor changes in goals, roles, and responsibilities?
- What kinds of support do different learners need?

> ◆ What expectations do members have for the group and for one another?
>
> ◆ What larger environments have an impact on our learning, and how will we address those impacts together?
>
> ◆ How will we monitor the documents, journals, reflections, or portfolios of our learning?

(Adapted from Collay et al., 1998.)

In one learning community, different members assumed the responsibility for initially learning a specific technology tool or software systems. The members became proficient and developed applications that were appropriate to the teams' units. Then, each "expert" on the team taught the technology and its application to their teammates. The time to learn five new technological advances was drastically reduced, and the integration into teaching was much more effective than if each member had learned on their own.

Interdependence is also supported by using the change cycle described in Chapter 2 to assure that PLCs honor adult learning needs and promote an effective change process. The cycle can be used at the PLC level, at the school level, and at the district level. When each level follows the change cycle, learning is reinforced through a common process and language—a double loop of learning (Senge, 2000) that reinforces interdependence of goals, learning, resources, and celebrations (Figure 5.4).

Figure 5.4. Double-Loop Learning Communities

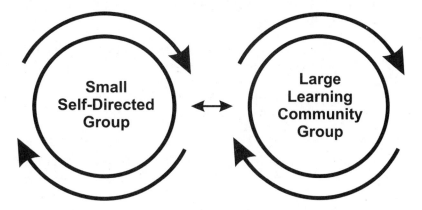

One PLC member provided a wonderful idea for systematizing the double-loop learning from year to year as new teachers joined the staff. At the first meeting of the school year, each PLC would share, both verbally and in a written summary, experiences they have had through the years and also ways in which they might contribute to the learning of others. In this way, the culture of learning and change was communicated to the new staff and reinforced among the existing staff. In addition, PLC groups could get new ideas about strategies to try with assurance that there was a ready human resource they could tap immediately. This is a wonderful way to celebrate, communicate, and build a cohesive change culture.

Time is a precious commodity in an educator's day. Learning community meetings hold greater value to participants when conversations stay focused. The Change cycle can become the focus for many professional development activities in PLCs by using reflective questions to guide the thinking of the group through the change process. Discussions need to progress rather rapidly through the change quadrants by assessing needs, addressing new learning, moving to application, and finally reflecting on results and future implications. The following table of learning community activities and discussion questions (Figure 5.5) can be used as a reference to focus PLC work on the stages in the Change cycle. Each set of questions helps participants move through understanding, internalizing, operationalizing, and evaluating changes in the professional learning-community change cycle.

**Figure 5.5. Learning Community Questions
to Focus Discussion on the Change Cycle**

PLC Activity	Learning Community Questions to Focus Discussion on the Change Cycle
Professional Growth on Teacher Evaluation Rubric	1. What area of the professional educator evaluation rubric will be the focus of our learning? How will this focus help student learning? 2. What evidence do we have about our current performance in this area? 3. What do we need to know and be able to demonstrate to increase our performance to the next level on the rubric? 4. What resources do we need to increase our performance in this area? 5. What actions do we plan, and what evidence will we collect to demonstrate our improvement in this area?

Read and/ or Share Books or Articles	1. What can we learn from this book or article that would help us with our student learning needs?
	2. What can we learn from this book or article that would help us in our professional or learning community needs?
	3. What would we like to know that is not included in this book or article?
	4. What actions or activities do we want to plan based on this book or article?
	5. What challenges would we face in taking these actions?
Discuss a Video	1. What can we learn from this video that would help us with our student learning needs?
	2. What can we learn from this video that would help us in our learning community efforts?
	3. What was missing in this video that we'd like to know more about?
	4. How can this video be useful tour team?
	5. What actions do we want to take based on this video?
Develop a Teaching Activity Together	1. What do we want this activity to accomplish for our students?
	2. What are some things about this activity that might work well with our students or not work well with our students?
	3. What do we need to do to make this activity successful?
	4. When will team members use this activity?
	5. What student information will be collect during or following this activity?
Peer Observations and Coaching	1. What did we want this lesson to accomplish for students?
	2. What teaching strategies did our colleague use?
	3. What worked well; what did not work well?
	4. What was the student response to the lesson and strategy?
	5. What are our plans for trying this lesson or strategy again?

Apply New Strategies	1. What do we want this strategy to accomplish for student learning?
	2. What worked well while using this strategy?
	3. What frustrations are we experiencing in using this strategy?
	4. How did students respond to the use of this strategy?
	5. What are our plans for using this strategy again?
Examine Student Work	1. Which student work protocol will be used to examine the student work?
	2. What evidence of student learning do we have?
	3. What learning should be taking place that is not taking place?
	4. Does the assignment produce the intended results?
	5. What conclusions or recommendations can we make about this assignment?
Plan for the Next Meeting	1. What do we want to accomplish at the next meeting?
	2. What are the major tasks that need to be done before the next meeting?
	3. Who will be responsible for each task?
	4. When and where will we meet?
	5. Who will be the recorder for the next meeting?
Assess Learning Community Progress	1. What tasks did we plan to accomplish by this time?
	2. Which tasks are completed and which remain to be accomplished?
	3. In what priority shall we accomplished the remaining tasks?
	4. What skills and resources will we need to accomplish the remaining tasks?
	5. What are our next steps?

Reflect on the Meeting	1. What did we accomplish today?
	2. What did we learn about students today?
	3. What did we learn about our professional practice today?
	4. What plans for action did we make today?
	5. What insights did we gain from each another today?

(Adapted from Murphy & Lick, 1998.)

What Strategies Can Increase Interpersonal and Group Skills in Professional Learning Communities?

Effective interpersonal interactions are essential for groups to work interdependently. Conflicts in PLCs typically arise because people do not know how to communicate effectively with one another. Hostility arises from miscommunication and misunderstanding. Groups must learn interpersonal communication skills and group processes that assure that decisions are made effectively and that problems are resolved as they arise. In this way, conflicts and hostility are avoided and groups become "dream teams." We developed the fifth and sixth innovation maps (Figures 5.6 and 5.7) to focus attention on the development of interpersonal and group-processing skills. These innovation maps parallel the previous maps with guiding questions, components, and levels of implementation.

Figure 5.6. PLC Implementation Innovation Map Five—Interpersonal Interactions

Guiding questions for increasing implementation levels:
- What is our role in communicating with colleagues?
- What are different ways in which we typically communicate with colleagues?
- How do we assess individual and group effectiveness in communications with colleagues?

Interpersonal Interactions

Interpersonal Interactions Categories	Level 1 Implementation		Level 2 Implementation		Level 3 Implementation	
	Teacher	Leader	Teacher	Leader	Teacher	Leader
Interpersonal skills Assesses, selects, learns, and uses effective interpersonal skills to support	Develops awareness of interpersonal skills needed for effective group functioning.	Determines interpersonal skill needs of staff. Develops initial awareness of need for effective interpersonal skills.	Selects, learns, and uses effective interpersonal skills.	Facilitates assessment, selection, and teaching of needed interpersonal skills.	Selects and consistently uses a broad range of effective interpersonal skills.	Assesses individual and group interpersonal skills to assure effective use of a broad range of interpersonal skills.
Interpersonal interactions Monitors, adjusts, and coaches effective interpersonal interactions.	Commits to learning and reflecting on personal and group interactions to improve PLC work.	Teaches and monitors initial interpersonal interactions.	Monitors individual and group interpersonal interactions to identify improvement areas.	Monitors and coaches for improvements in individual and group interpersonal interactions.	Consistently reflects on and refines interpersonal interactions to improve PLC work.	Coaches for consistent use, reflection, and refinement of effective interpersonal interactions.

Figure 5.7. Innovation Map Six—Group Processing

Guiding questions for increasing implementation levels:

- How do we organize ourselves for teaching and learning?
- How do we go about finding out how our colleagues prefer to share information and communication?
- How do our communications with colleagues increase our understanding about how to increase student learning?

Group Processing

Group Processing Categories	Level 1 Implementation		Level 2 Implementation		Level 3 Implementation	
	Teacher	Leader	Teacher	Leader	Teacher	Leader
Group-processing skills Assesses, learns, and implements group process skills into PLCs.	Develops awareness of group-processing skills needed for effective function of PLC groups.	Determines initial group-processing needs of staff. Develops awareness of the need for group-processing skills.	Selects, learns, and uses effective group-processing skills.	Facilitates assessment, selection, and learning of effective group-processing skills.	Selects and consistently uses a broad range of group-processing skills.	Assesses individual and group use of a broad range of effective group-processing skills.
Group-processing use Uses group reflections to discuss, draft, and implement changes in the way the group works.	Commits to learning and reflecting on group processes to improve the PLC work.	Teaches and monitors initial use of group-processing skills.	Uses group processing to discuss, draft, and implement changes in the way the group works.	Monitors, teaches, and coaches use of group processing to implement changes in group work.	Consistently reflects and refines group processes to discuss, draft, and implement improvements in the group's work.	Coaches for consistent use, reflection, and refinement of group processing to improve the group's work.

Again, we invite you to take a moment to assess the level of implementation your school has demonstrated. What evidence do you have that your teachers are at this level? What evidence do you have that you, as the leader, are performing at this level? What evidence would you need to move to the next level? How might the answers to the guiding questions change from level to level and help teachers and leaders develop greater interpersonal and group-processing skills? What other types of evidence might you have or need in your school or district that demonstrates the levels of implementation for interpersonal and group-processing skills?

Interpersonal and social skills can be selected, taught, practiced, and assessed. Johnson et al. (2006) identified four stages of group development and the interpersonal skills needed in each stage. We adapted the interpersonal skills to those we find important in PLCs (Figure 5.8).

Figure 5.8. Stages of Professinal Learning Community Group Development with Interpersonal Skills

Forming	Functioning	Formulating	Fermenting
◆ Regularly attends meetings and is on time ◆ Stays with group, no wandering or off-topic conversations ◆ Uses a respectful voice in the group ◆ Listens and takes turns when talking ◆ Respects rights of others ◆ Positive about working in group ◆ Willing to help others ◆ Follows directions ◆ Shows courtesy to others	◆ Clarifies goals ◆ Gives direction to groups' work ◆ Contributes ideas and opinions ◆ Requests ideas and opinions from others ◆ Encourages participation of others ◆ Paraphrases ◆ Relieves tension appropriately ◆ Supports others, gives recognition, praises ideas	◆ Summarizes and integrates ideas of others ◆ Seeks accuracy and corrects errors ◆ Relates new learning to old ◆ Helps group recall and record ◆ Checks for understanding ◆ Makes covert reasoning or assumptions overt	◆ Criticizes ideas, not people ◆ Differentiates members' ideas; Integrates members' ideas ◆ Asks for reasoning or justification ◆ Extends other's reasoning ◆ Probes, asks complex questions ◆ Uses protocols (decision-making, problem-solving, student work) to explore and understand issues or problems

Leaders can observe PLCs to determine the stage of development of a team and determine which interpersonal skills are needed to improve their functioning as a group. One principal simply asked each PLC to highlight the skills they felt they consistently used well and to circle the skills they thought they could improve on. This allowed the principal to focus his observations of PLC meetings and to develop a plan for interpersonal skill development for the year.

Once the interpersonal skills are identified, leaders can systematically teach the social skills. The protocol for teaching social skills involves (a) clarifying synonyms for the skill, (b) defining the skill, (c) sharing ideas about where the skill is used in everyday life, (d) identifying what the skill looks like and sounds like in use, (e) defining the steps for using the skill, (f) practicing the skill, and (g) assessing the skill. A sample lesson demonstrating the steps in this protocol appears in Figure 5.9.

Figure 5.9. Interpersonal and/or Social Skill Development Lesson

Interpersonal skill: Encourage participation.	
Synonyms: Seeks ideas, asks for ideas, praises sharing, invites others to join the conversation.	
Definition: To use actions and words that invite others to join in the group activities.	
Where do we use this in everyday life: Conversations at the dinner table, play groups for our children, sporting activities, clubs, or organizations.	

Looks Like	Sounds Like
Eye contact; Lean forward; Making space at the table for others; Point to others to get them to share	Ask questions directed at another; Invitation to join and share; Friendly tone of voice; Praise for ideas

Steps:

1. Make space at the table for each member.
2. Make eye contact with each member.
3. Invite members to share ideas and join the activity.
4. Use a friendly tone of voice.
5. Ask questions and ask for ideas from members.
6. Praise members for sharing ideas.

Practice and/or application: Use a simple activity to practice the use of the skill and then use the skill in the PLC group.

Review or revise steps: When you use the skill discuss the steps used and review or revise ideas about what the skill looks like and sounds like to reinforce the skill use.
Assess: Group review helps the group assess the use of the skill, but leaders should also watch for the proficient use of social skills and invite groups to share their experiences in using the skill.

Group processing focuses on how groups make decisions, stay focused, manage group interactions, and deal with group conflicts. Groups who define the processes by which they will address these four areas are better able to self-monitor actions and make adjustments as needed.

Making Decisions—Will you use majority rule or consensus? How will you determine the level of support for a decision? What are strategies you will use to develop decisions? How could you use brainstorming, listing criteria, affinity mapping, data dumps, or best and worst case scenarios to improve decisions?

Staying Focused—What is the mission and vision for the group? How will agendas be planned? How will you assure that members adhere to the agenda and it's time limits? How will you capture the discussions and ideas in the minutes?

Managing Group Interactions—How will you develop and monitor group norms? Whose responsibility is it to manage group interactions and what interventions will be used to redirect interactions? How will you facilitate group development through the normal stages of forming, storming, norming, and performing? How will you monitor nonverbal interactions that interfere with communication?

Dealing with Group Conflicts—How will you identify problem meeting behaviors? Whose responsibility is it to address group conflicts? How will you share perspectives about the conflict? How will you surface assumptions that are leading to conflict? How much time will you permit for venting before members are redirected to finding options for change? How will you develop options for resolution of conflicts? How will you turn options in to action plans? How will you monitor action plans to assure successful resolution of the conflict? (Scheffert, Anderson, & Anderson, 1999)

A key way for leaders to ensure that group processing occurs in PLCs is to require documentation of learning, reflections, and successes in an agenda or log. The questions listed with making decisions, staying focused, managing group interactions, and dealing with group conflicts can be included in meeting agendas for reflection by PLC teams. An additional way in which groups can process the academic and social activities in a PLC is through the use of the Critical Incident Questionnaire, adapted from the work of Stephen Brookfield (1995). The questions help groups identify the actual incidents during meetings that contribute to or detract from learning. The questions in Figure 5.10 can surface incidents. Once the incident is identified, the group can discuss and develop processes to reinforce positive incidents or reduce negative incidents.

Figure 5.10. Critical Incident Questionnaire

1. When did you feel most connected today?

2. When did you feel most disconnected today?

3. When were you most assisted in your learning today?

4. When were you puzzled by something someone said or did?

5. When did you feel most engaged in the learning today?

6. When did you contribute to your learning?

7. When did you contribute to the learning of others in your group?

Other resources that are useful in developing interpersonal and group-processing skills include the following.

♦ Johnson et al. (2006) provide effective instruction and examples on both interpersonal skill and group-processing development in *Active Learning: Cooperation in the College Classroom.*

♦ Barkley et al. (2005) provide strategies that support collaborative learning for adults in *Collaborative Learning Techniques.*

♦ Marzano and Pickering (1997) provide instruction and graphic organizers on how to make decisions, solve problems, invent solutions, or investigate issues in *Dimensions of Learning.*

♦ Scheffert et al. (1999) provides resources for learning group facilitation skills, agenda design, managing interactions, and managing group conflict in *Facilitation Resources*, Volumes 1 through 7.

How Can We Ensure Individual and Group Accountability?

Professional learning communities need group and individual goals and systems for documenting goal performance to assure success. Reliance on a single group goal with reporting that aggregates the performance at the group level allows individuals to abdicate their personal responsibility toward the goal. The high achieving members of the group tend to carry the free-riders. When this happens, the group does not increase group capability or collective efficacy. The capability and efficacy is still limited to selected members who may develop resentment toward the free-riders. Goal setting and accountability must include both group goals and individual goals in support of the group goals. Accountability reports should include information on the group goal, the individual goal, the individual and group roles and responsibilities for activities aligned to the goals, and individual and group data on goal attainment. Action plans for PLCs should define individual and group objectives; which person is responsible; the how, when, and where the action will be conducted; and expected results.

Accountability is best assured through the development of goals that are specific, measurable, accountable, realistic, and timely (SMART). Somewhere in the last 10 years "accountable" was changed to "achievable," which is actually the same as "realistic." If the accountability function of a SMART goal is missing, members of a PLC can say they tried but that the goal was not entirely their responsibility. Therefore, failure to achieve the goal can be blamed on someone else not doing their part. Relational responsibility requires both individual and group accountability to the SMART goals.

In addition to identifying the SMART goals for student learning, we suggest that PLCs develop parallel SMART goals for teacher and/or leader learning, PLC relational components, and PLC structural components to assure that members in the PLC are accountable to their own learning and to factors that will assure the successful functioning of the group.

After reading the book *Learning Circles* (Collay et al., 1998), one of our PLC members focused on a particular sentence in the text that said "[L]earning circles are for personal and professional development not for institutional management." She reflected, "I think that sentence is so important. I have only been thinking of PLC's as means of improving student achievement. I have not been focused on what we as professionals need for our own growth. I know that as I think of possible career changes, I will be looking for environments where this growth can happen. I also think that our teaching staff was not open to pay for performance ideas, because they did not see the potential for their own benefit as professionals."

See Figure 5.11 for a template that can be used to design SMART goals that serve student goals as well as personal and professional development goals. By using the SMART goals template, we focus on three things: what is good for the student, what is good for the group, and what is good for the individual educator. This helps educators better understand the win-win nature of their actions and therefore enhances both commitment to action and a positive, professional work environment.

Figure 5.11. SMART Goal Process

SMART: Specific, measurable, accountable, realistic, and timely.

SMART Goal: _____

	Student Learning and Growth	Professional Learning and Growth	PLC Cultural Components	PLC Structural Components
Specific				
Measurable				
Accountable				
Realistic				
Timely				

To help you see how this expanded use of SMART goals might look, we created an example (Figure 5.12) by taking an actual building SMART goal and breaking it apart to examine the student growth goal, the companion professional growth SMART goal that would support the student growth goal, and the cultural and structural SMART goals that would support the professional growth goal in the PLC.

Figure 5.12. Sample SMART Goal Process

SMART Goal for Leading PLCs

SMART: Specific, measurable, accountable, realistic, and timely.

SMART goal: Seventy-five percent of students in grades 2 through 5 will have a word recognition and/or vocabulary strand score at or above the norm for their grade level on the Northwest Evaluation Association (NWEA) test at the end of the year. Currently, 67 percent of students are scoring at that level.

	Student Learning and Growth	Professional Learning and Growth	PLC Cultural Components	PLC Structural Components
Specific	Word recognition and/or vocabulary strand Grades 2–5 NWEA test.	Learn several word recognition and/or vocabulary strategies that can be used in small, differentiated groups.	Use our feedback form to conduct more frequent analysis of group processes.	Make time in each PLC agenda to share professional growth using lessons and videos and for group processing.
Measurable	At or above the norm for the grade level on the NWEA test.	Vocabulary strategies and small group differentiated practices are documented in lesson plans and visible in video-taped lessons.	Group-processing questions answered with plan to address needs.	Agendas designate time for additional SMART goal discussions.

	Student Learning and Growth	Professional Learning and Growth	PLC Cultural Components	PLC Structural Components
Accountable	75% of students in grades 2–5 will be at or above grade-level norm.	Lesson plans and personal video analysis of the use of strategies and small group differentiation are shared and discussed in PLCs.	Individuals answer independently and then the group seeks consensus and makes plans for changes.	Feedback form documents discussions and actions regarding professional growth and group processing.
Realistic	Currently 67% of students are at-taining this level of performance. (We don't know why 75% feels attainable.)	Strategies in text; Share new strategies in PLC; Previous professional de-velopment on differentiation	Have used group processing a few times already and now want to make it a common practice.	The 2-hour PLC time will allow time to process the additional SMART goals.
Timely	By the end of the year.	Lessons and video analysis shared once a month.	Every 2 weeks during PLC.	Each agenda and feedback form, every 2 weeks.

The PLC action plan form (Figure 5.13) can be used to effectively document individual and group goals, actions, and results that arise from the SMART goal process. Goals that are broken down into objectives, actions, persons responsible, timelines, and expected results can be clearly aligned to clarify expectations and accountability. We have seen PLCs use these maps at the beginning and the end of meetings to celebrate progress and clearly identify personal and group responsibilities for next steps.

Figure 5.13. Professional Learning Communities Action Plan

PLC or Leadership Committee Members: _____

Mission: _____

Vision: _____

Goal(s): _____

Objectives	Activities	People Responsible	Timeline	Completion Date/Results

In the movie *A Beautiful Mind*, economist John Nash is awarded the Nobel Prize in Economics for his revision of the Theory of Governing Dynamics (Howard, 2002). In a previous explanation of the theory, the father of modern economics, John Smith, argued that in competition, individual ambition serves the common wealth. John Nash's work, however, revealed that the best results do not come from everyone doing what is best for them. The best result comes from everyone doing what's best for themselves and the group. Professional learning communities by their very nature are governed by this revised theory and the SMART goal template assures that we attend to these dynamics.

We developed the seventh innovation map (Figure 5.14) to focus attention on the development of independent and group accountability. This innovation map parallels the previous maps with guiding questions, components, and levels of implementation.

Figure 5.14. Innovation Map Seven—Individual and Group Accountability

Guiding questions for increasing implementation levels:

- What are our roles or responsibilities in documenting student learning?
- What are our roles or responsibilities in documenting professional growth?
- What evidence would best demonstrate our individual and group accountability to student learning and professional growth?

Individual and Group Accountability

Accountability	Level 1 Implementation		Level 2 Implementation		Level 3 Implementation	
Categories	**Teacher**	**Leader**	**Teacher**	**Leader**	**Teacher**	**Leader**
Individual accountability Accounts for individual goals, learning, actions, and results. Fulfills individual roles and responsibilities for improved student learning and professional growth.	Identifies evidence might use to document individual goals, learning, actions, results, and fulfillment of roles and responsibilities for improved student learning and professional growth.	Develops commitment to using evidence to document individual goals, learning, actions, results, and fulfillment of roles and responsibilities for improved student learning and professional growth.	Collects summative evidence to document individual goals, learning, actions, results, and fulfillment of individual roles and responsibilities for improved student learning and professional growth.	Supports, assesses, and coaches the collection of summative evidence to document individual goals, learning, actions, results, and fulfillment of individual roles and responsibilities for improved student learning and professional growth.	Uses multiple forms of formative and summative evidence to document student learning and professional growth. Reflects on evidence to plan future improvements.	Assesses and coaches individuals to consistently use multiple forms of formative and summative evidence to document student learning and professional growth as well as plans for future improvements.

Figure 5.14. Innovation Map Seven (continued)

Individual and Group Accountability

Accountability	Level 1 Implementation		Level 2 Implementation		Level 3 Implementation	
Categories	Teacher	Leader	Teacher	Leader	Teacher	Leader
Group accountability Accounts for the alignment of group goals, learning, and actions toward collective results. Fulfills group roles and responsibilities for improved student learning and group professional growth.	Identifies PLC group evidence for possible use to collectively document goals, learning, actions, results, and fulfillment of roles and responsibilities for improving student learning and professional growth.	Develops commitment to using evidence to document PLC group goals, learning, actions, results, and fulfillment of roles and responsibilities for improving student learning and professional growth.	Collects summative PLC group evidence to document goals, learning, actions, results, and fulfillment of roles and responsibilities for improving student learning and professional growth.	Supports, assesses, and coaches the collection of PLC group summative evidence to document group goals, learning, actions, results, and fulfillment of roles and responsibilities for improved student learning and professional growth.	Uses multiple forms of PLC formative and summative evidence to document student learning and professional growth. Reflects on PLC group evidence to plan future improvements.	Assesses and coaches PLC groups to consistently use multiple forms of formative and summative evidence to document student learning and professional growth as well as plans for future improvements.

Again, we invite you to take a moment to assess the level of implementation your school has demonstrated. What evidence do you have that your teachers are at this level? What evidence do you have that you, as the leader, are performing at this level? What evidence would you need to move to the next level? How might the answers to the guiding questions change from level to level and help teachers and leaders develop greater independent and group accountability? What other types of evidence might you have or need in your school or district that demonstrates the level of implementation for independent and group accountability.

When PLC members develop their relational skills using the innovation maps in this chapter, they also support the development of a culturally responsive, inclusive learning environment for themselves and others.

- ◆ Judgment of teaching practices is suspended to focus on changes in behavior that support educator learning
- ◆ Positive interaction skills are not assumed but are actively taught to educators and leaders.
- ◆ Norms and processes reflect a value of differences and are culturally sensitive. Educators monitor norms and group processes frequently.
- ◆ All educators feel valued by other educators and are challenged by the high expectations of other educators.
- ◆ Educators reflect on the impact of actions on each other as well as on their students.
- ◆ Educators accept and appreciate different ideas, opinions, and learning styles of other educators.
- ◆ Professional development practices do not conflict with values, beliefs, or cultural practices of educators.
- ◆ A variety of assessments are used to document accountability by individuals and groups to ensure that the same standards are applied with all educators.

The more that educators experience such an effective environment, the more they will be able to create culturally responsive, inclusive environments for their students (Singleton & Linton, 2006). By working on their own relationships, they will learn to develop effective learning environments for their students.

Post Vignette

Based on the information in this chapter and PLC Implementation Innovation Maps Four, Five, Six, and Seven, we invite you to analyze the following vignette and determine: (a) the level of implementation involving interdependence, interpersonal skills, group processing, and accountability for teachers, (b) the level of implementation involving interdependence, interpersonal skills, group processing, and accountability for the leader

(Teresa), and (c) the next steps needed for the teachers and the leader to move forward in the implementation of their PLCs.

Teresa's principal PLC studied cooperative and collaborative learning and systematically incorporated the practices for interdependence, interpersonal skills, group processing, and accountability for individual and group goals into their work. This helped Teresa assess her own teacher PLCs for appropriate use of interpersonal and group-processing skills. She determined that all teams needed to have conversations about what would build their teams and what would destroy teams. At a faculty meeting, teams discussed a set of questions to determine how they would sustain their interdependence. The small groups then shared their commitments with the whole school.

Teresa observed her "dream team" to understand how they used effective interpersonal skills and then observed other teams in the school to determine how to build the capacity of her staff to work effectively with one another. She selected two social skills that needed improvement and asked her "dream team" to lead the faculty in mini-lessons for each skill, followed by practice in their PLCs. She closely monitored the work of her "team from hell" and helped them examine their interactions. Their discussions became more respectful but were still controlled and guarded. They agreed to work collaboratively when face to face but were still working more independently to achieve their group goal. Teresa hoped that with continued practice they would learn to develop more interdependence of roles and responsibilities.

Teresa worked with her leadership team to develop a PLC log that would document the groups' SMART goals, individual goals, specific accountability plans, and reflections about how the groups were processing their work and interactions. Her troubled PLC was able to successfully compose a SMART goal with aligned individual goals and had started to design action plans. They still struggled to process their plans, interactions, or reflections about how they were doing as a PLC, but ceased threatening to file a union grievance for the work they were doing.

Vignette Analysis

Although she has recognized a need to improve interdependence, placing her at level 1, Teresa has yet to monitor interdependence or establish a commitment to a continuous improvement process. She might help her staff understand how a cycle of learning in community can support their professional growth and change. Providing reflection questions on the agendas of PLCs could lead teachers in the practice of the cycle as they become more familiar with the process of change. Teresa and some of her teachers are moving to level 2 on the Interpersonal Skills Innovation Map.

Her troubled PLC team remains at level 1 of the Interdependence Innovation Map in spite of the fact that Teresa is operating at level 2 on the Interpersonal Skills Innovation map. Teresa could encourage discussions to clarify interdependent roles, responsibilities, and resources that might help this team communicate better. She could also share feedback with each member individually about social skills that could be improved. The teachers and Teresa are at level 1 on both the Group Processing Innovation Map and the Individual and Group Accountability Innovation Map. Teresa will be able to use the PLC logs to assess group processing and accountability practices so that she can monitor and coach improvements in the future, thereby moving herself and her staff to level 2. Teresa effectively averted union action by building relationships, positive interactions, and enhanced accountability.

Reflecting Forward

Use the guiding questions for increasing implementation levels for the rubric(s) associated with this chapter to explore beliefs, assumptions, practices, and evidence that can help you move forward.

- At what level of implementation are teachers and leaders?
- What evidence do you have that documents this level of implementation for teachers and leaders?
- What evidence would you need to move to the next level of implementation?
- What new learning and resources (physical and human) would you need to move to the next level of implementation?
- What practices would you need to implement to move to the next level of implementation?
- What evidence would you collect and reflect upon to assess progress to the next level of implementation?
- Who will you involve when reflecting on your new learning?
- With whom will you collaborate to improve the learning or implement the new learning across your school and/or district?

You may find the following form (Figure 5.15) helpful as you process the guiding questions:

Figure 5.15. Guiding Questions Process Form

Where are we, and what evidence do we have of our current level of implementation?	Where do we want to be, and what evidence do we need to move to the next level of implementation?

6

The Learning Is in the Questions

Vignette 6

In Teresa's district, new teachers are formally observed three times per year for the first three years, while tenured teachers are observed once every three years. Observations typically engender fear of judgment rather than openness to improvements. Teresa has noted that the teachers most suspicious of observation are also most resistant to new learning and PLCs. When she visits PLC meetings, conversations become shallow and abnormally positive. Everything is terrific.

How could she increase her ability to monitor, assess, and guide future professional growth and PLC implementation with limited access? She attended a workshop to learn about classroom walk-throughs and returned knowing the process would increase access issues. She wanted to ask questions following observations that would encourage team reflection and lead to changes in practice. She wanted her questions to develop interdependence among teachers rather than dependence on her. Teresa wanted to improve her instructional coaching and she wanted teachers to observe and coach each other. How could they use observations and coaching to inform them on the success of their PLC development?

Guiding Questions

- ◆ Why is coaching essential for effective PLC development?
- ◆ What are the roles and responsibilities of an effective coach?
- ◆ How can we design coaching questions that promote change in beliefs and practices?
- ◆ What are some approaches to coaching that can be used in PLCs?

Why is Coaching Essential for Effective Professional Learning Community Development?

A key reason for emphasizing coaching as a professional development tool is to promote change in teacher practices. Research by Joyce and Showers, in *Student Achievement through Staff Development* (1988, 2002; Figure 6.1), reveals that only through the use of coaching are teachers able to achieve high levels of concept understanding, skill attainment, and ability to apply and solve problems. The most telling difference is in the ability to apply learning to real problems in classrooms.

Figure 6.1. Joyce and Showers Research on Impact of Coaching on Professional Learning

Components of Training	Concept Understanding	Skill Attainment	Apply/ Problem Solve
Present theory	85%	15%	5–10%
Modeling	85%	18%	5–10%
Practice with low risk feedback	85%	80%	10–15%
Coaching ◆ Study teams ◆ Peer visits ◆ Reflective practice	90%	90%	80–90%

We learned in Chapter 2 that adult learning and change were enhanced through social transactions, self-reflection, and self-directed behavior toward professional standards (Foord, 2004). Coaching with questions serves all of these important functions. Coaching promotes reflection about teaching practices by asking questions that probe and clarify the teacher's understanding and application. Assumptions about teaching and learning are uncovered, and beliefs and values about student and teacher learning are examined. Both coach and teacher experience cognitive growth in the process as they construct understanding about teaching standards and practices together. Effective coaching builds trust in the coaching process through nonjudgmental, accepting questions that encourage a continuous cycle of new learning, application, and reflection.

Coaching also embodies the elements of cooperative learning, permitting us to engage in the process of cooperative learning with teachers even when they are not formal members of each PLC. Through coaching, we engage in face-to-face interactions that develop interdependent goals for improving teaching and learning. The coaching process depends on effective interpersonal skills and a trusting process to maintain the viability of the coach and teacher relationship. The coach may have individual goals but also must support the goals of the coaching partnership if it is to continue. Coaching permits us to actively model the skills of cooperative learning for teachers who, in turn, learn from this effective modeling.

Each of the innovation maps in this book relies on coaching by leaders to assure PLC implementation at level 2 and level 3. This chapter contains several practices and resources designed to support our use of coaching to increase teacher professional practices and implementation of PLCs.

What Are the Roles and Responsibilities of an Effective Coach?

Just as teachers must commit to their roles and responsibilities in PLCs and practice their way into effective use of interpersonal and group processing skills, so too, must we, as leaders, commit to our roles and responsibilities as coaches and practice our way into fluid use of effective coaching questions. Leaders play a crucial role in the successful development of high-functioning PLCs through effective application of instructional coaching.

Principals are increasingly told they must be the instructional leaders or coaches in their schools. There are a wide variety of approaches that have been suggested. Some approaches focus on collecting data and providing specific feedback. Some approaches focus on observing specific indicators of excellence that are present in a classroom and guiding professional development to increase those indicators. Some focus on the leader directing the conversations, whereas others seek to have the teachers direct the conversations about improvements in instruction. In some approaches the leader constructs evidence of teacher proficiency, and in others the teacher constructs their own understanding of proficiency.

We have found that instructional coaching is a primary factor in increasing the implementation level of PLCs and that using questions is the key to effective coaching. In our work with PLCs, coaching questions have played a central role in improving teacher practices for four reasons:

1. Effective use of coaching questions increases teacher learning by broadening perceptions to pursue new opportunities or options.
2. Effective use of coaching questions focuses conversations on essential changes in practices.
3. Effective use of coaching questions increases commitment to change.
4. Effective use of coaching questions distributes responsibility for change among all educators.

The innovation maps in this book serve as inquiry guides in the development of PLCs. Each map begins with essential guiding questions designed to surface assumptions and prompt new learning about the work of PLCs. In addition, each of the innovation maps requires coaching starting at the second level of implementation. Simply put, without coaching for inquiry, we do not believe that PLCs can move beyond level 1 of implementation, and this coaching depends on the leader's ability to design and use effective coaching questions. We will explore this crucial skill in the next section, but before we do, we offer a few other guiding roles and responsibilities for the coaching leader.

Costa and Garmston (2005) suggest that effective cognitive coaches: Diagnose and envision desired stages for others; construct and use clear and precise language in the facilitation of others' cognitive development; devise an overall strategy through which individuals will move themselves toward desired states; maintain faith in the potential for continued movement toward more autonomous states of mind and behavior; and possess a belief in their own capacity to serve as an empowering catalyst of others' growth. Ultimately, practice with coaching leads to teacher self-coaching to improve professional practices.

We invite you to incorporate the following coaching roles and responsibilities (Figure 6.2) into your own practice as you coach educators and PLCs.

Figure 6.2. Coaching Roles and Responsibilities

Roles	Responsibilities
Initiator	Sets up expectations and opportunities for coaching to occur. Helps educators enter into discussions with themselves, their colleagues, and their leaders.
Trust builder	Selects coaching questions and uses actions that promote positive presuppositions about the adult's capability to produce effective results. Develops self-trust in educators so that they can find the answer within themselves.
Educator not evaluator	Promotes focus on learning, options, and opportunities not judgment or evaluation. Promotes deep, reflective thinking and inquiry but does not guarantee or provide answers. Uses questions to open doors to new perceptions and viewpoints.
Story seeker	Invites storytelling to translate new experiences into new learning, which in turn solidifies the learning. Uses stories as the method for new learning, reflection on learning, assessment of learning, and celebration of learning. Storytelling is used to reculture educators, education, and schools.
Professional mirror	Develops the professional self-image of educators consistent with excellence and efficacy in the profession. Develops both self- and collective efficacy among educators.
Diversity director	Differentiates questions based on the experiences, competence, and stages of change needed by each adult.
Distributor	Distributes coaching opportunities and responsibilities among educators and in doing so, distributes learning among faculty.

A brief rationale for each role and responsibility follows to explain their importance.

Initiator

Education is plagued by privatized practice, and educators do not initiate coaching opportunities. A "don't ask, don't tell" mentality pervades schools, and there is really no systemic incentive for educators to ask questions and seek coaching other than some concern for results based on yearly accountability tests. We must break this pattern by initiating both the expectation and the opportunities for questions and coaching. Naturally, educators will need to know why we are changing expectations and what the benefit will be for them. Anxiety will give way to awareness and positive anticipation when educators understand that the purpose is to help them find the answers within themselves, their practice, their colleagues' practices, and the profession.

Trust Builder

Questions that presume that the educator is competent reinforce the belief that the educator has many choices and is in control. This enhances feelings of trust in themselves and in the process of discovery the question creates. The fewer the number of perceived choices, the more out of control an educator may assess him or herself to be. Questions that promote positive presupposition assume that effective actions are possible, the educator is responsible, able, and has many choices of action (Goldberg, 1998). Consider the following questions and the underlying messages that they communicate. How might each weaken trust in self and in the process of coaching? How could each question be rewritten as a question presuming individual or collective competence?

- ◆ What were you thinking when you argued with Sam in front of the class about sitting in his assigned seat?
- ◆ Why did you spend an hour lecturing when the students seemed to already understand the concept?
- ◆ Did you even consider that your students are 10th graders when you had them coloring?
- ◆ Do you ever show up for faculty meetings?

Goldberg (1998) suggests that educators should ask the question, "'What can I do?' This question, built on the presuppositions that capability and options are available, automatically gives the individual a range of possibilities whereas yes/no questions give him only one" (p. 22). If we change the question to "What can we do?," it generates positive presuppositions of capability and options for a group and therefore builds collective efficacy. What are the characteristics of a question that builds trust? What words, phrases, or structures in the question produce trust? Later in this chapter we provide examples of safe, trusting, and yet cognitively challenging questions that can be used to coach. When we act consistently to ask safe, respectful, questions that demonstrate positive beliefs about capabilities and permit many choices or possibilities, educators can learn to trust the coaching process. The process is about educators finding answers to the questions, not the leader finding the answer for them.

Educator Not Evaluator

Often the questions we ask other educators represent answers to our internal speculation about them. We judge them and then we use questions to supply answers to our judgment, hoping the answer will confirm our judgment. How can we alter our selection of questions to be nonjudgmental and enlist the educator in self-assessment of their practice for learning? (Goldberg, 1998; Stiggins et al., 2006)

Story Seeker

As we learned in Chapter 2, adult learning is enhanced when it is based on experience, is socially constructed, and when it is self-directed. Encouraging adults to tell their professional story is an effective way to support all

> Storytelling increases the number of comparisons of new experiences to prior experiences for adults and therefore increases learning and retention.

three adult needs and contributes to their learning and even their intelligence. Work in the area of neurolinguistic programming and intelligence support the importance of narrative storytelling and intelligence. Schank (1990) sums up the theory by stating that "what we know is embodied in what we tell and what we tell strongly determines what we know. We know what we tell, and we tell what we know" (p. 17). Assessment of what is known, either by the teacher or leader, is enhanced by conversation or storytelling and in telling the stories with a trusted coach, guiding the clarification and enhancement of the story, our understanding of what we know is increased. Shank (1990) explains why this process supports learning and intelligence.

> ...[T]hinking involves indexing. In order to assimilate a case, we must attach it someplace in memory. Information without access to that information is not information at all. Memory, in order to be effective, must contain both specific experiences (memories) and labels (memory traces). The more information we are provided with about a situation, the more places we can attach it to in memory. Thus, a story is useful because it comes with many indices. These indices may be locations, attitudes, quandaries, decisions, conclusions, or whatever. The more indices we have for a story that is being told, the more places it can reside in memory. Consequently, we are more likely to remember a story and to relate it to experiences already in memory. In other words, the more indices, the greater the number of comparisons with prior experiences and hence the greater the learning." (p. 11)

In their meta-analysis of research on instructional strategies that work, Marzano et al. (2001) identified the most significant gains in student learning occurred when teacher's involved students in the use of comparison and contrast and categorization. Storytelling increases the number of comparisons of new experiences to prior experiences for adults as well, and therefore increases learning and retention. In research conducted by Foord (2004), teachers involved in a year-long learning community were asked to tell stories about their best teaching experiences in a pre and post fashion. In addition, at monthly PLC meetings, teachers shared stories about the application of new teaching strategies to improve their practice and related their successes and concerns to a set of teaching standards. An appreciative inquiry approach (Cooperrider & Whitney, 2005) was used, focusing on what went well, worked, or was successful, to enhance the retention of the learning as a positive memory. The stories at the end of the learning community experience contained significantly more references to effective teaching practices, to teaching standards that were represented by those practices, and to explanations of why practices worked for students. Work by Sparks (2002) on positive deviance also demonstrates that when we look for stories and practices that are producing student achievement gains, we can learn much more about how to change our practices than if we focus on what is not working or on achievement problems. What would the teacher's lounge sound like if war stories were replaced with celebrations of success? How would teacher interactions change? Our guess is that instead of giving each other advice on how to fix problems, a form of judgment, educators would be asking questions about how to create the same successes in their own classrooms, engaging in professional, appreciative inquiry leading to self-directed changes in practice.

Cognitive coaching training (Costa & Garmston, 2005) is an effective way to learn how to facilitate this process. The coaching strategies allow us to seek the stories, guide the storyteller to explore

> What would the teacher's lounge sound like if war stories were replaced with celebrations of success?

different states of mind to compare and contrast and categorize the information in the story, and shape use of the experience for reflection, planning, or problem resolving.

Professional Mirror

As a coach we can serve as the mirror by which educators assess their own competence against professional standards and assess their teaching practices against national and state content standards for students. Coaching questions that direct thinking toward professional standards deepen awareness of and proficiency in those standards. When educators self-assess against clear profession standards, this also leads to self-motivation (Stiggins et al., 2006). Self-efficacy is increased because teachers reflect, assess, and plan for improvements in their image as a professional educator. When coaching questions are used in PLC groups or faculty meetings, the multiple stories of professional competence create a story of collective efficacy for professional behaviors, practices, and standards. A culture of competence is reflected back in the school mirror.

Diversity Director

Just as teachers must differentiate instruction for their students, the leader must differentiate their coaching and questions for educators based on their experience level, their teaching style or preference, and their current level of use of specific innovations or strategies. To enhance your coaching skills, we suggest exploring practices for differentiating supervision based on level of experience (Glickman, Gordon, & Ross-Gordon, 2004), differentiating supervision based on learning and teaching styles (Pajak, 2003), and differentiating expectations for change based on the levels of use of innovative practices (Hall & Hord, 2001).

Distributor

The effective leader finds ways to increase the number of coaches and coaching skills in their building or district. Sometimes this means developing a small set of mentor teachers who receive specialized training to serve as mentors and coaches for other teachers. In some districts, all teachers learn how to serve as peer coaches and the coaching becomes part of the work that is documented in PLCs. In one district, teachers initially coached each other by selecting and asking prepared coaching questions. Without additional training in coaching, they sometimes reverted to providing advice on how to change practices that led to discomfort and resistance. During the second year of coaching, teachers were advised to simply share observations about what they saw happening. The result was that coaching became much less valued because there was no cognitive challenge in the information. Educators were not helped in their thinking and reflecting about their practice. If we distribute coaching leadership, we must also be responsible for preparing and monitoring the effectiveness of the leadership. We will discuss additional ideas for developing and sustaining distributive leadership in Chapter 7.

How Can We Design Coaching Questions that Promote Change in Teacher Beliefs and Practices?

We know that one way to improve student learning is to increase effective questioning by teachers. Usually, this entails training in how to write questions at higher order thinking skill levels (HOTS). The questions should be open-ended with multiple possible answers. The questions should solicit extended explanations by students. The questions should be posed to all students with significant wait-time for response, and we should sample enough students to assess understanding by the group. Effective coaching questions are similar to effective teaching questions. They engage teachers in deep thinking about their practices and beliefs. They are open to multiple answers and require extended responses. We must wait for these thoughtful responses and sample enough teachers to know how deeply a practice is understood by individuals and the group.

Effective coaching questions possess additional qualities and characteristics that promote changes in beliefs and practices. Marilee Goldberg, in *The Art of the Question* (1998), explains the importance of using the right question:

> The structure of a question can put the speaker in particular worlds of perceptions, experience, and possibility. . . .While language structures reality, questions help structure language. (p. vii).... [A]sking the right questions helps clients [educators] think more clearly, take greater responsibility for themselves, and accomplish their goals more easily. They also communicate and engage in relationships more effectively. They consistently say they experience more happiness, freedom, and choice in their lives. Learning to ask the right question was like cracking the code on change. (p. x)

Change is one of the primary purposes of PLCs so finding the right questions to help us crack the code for change is a primary purpose in our coaching.

Questions that promote assessment for learning against a clear set of targets promote motivation to change and increase learning (Stiggins et al., 2006). Goldberg (1998) suggests that the coaching questions must shift thinking from judgment to learning. The focus of current accountability systems is on problems: What is not working, what is wrong, and who is at fault. This promotes questions of judgment and evaluation that paralyze change. Qualities for questions that contribute to assessment for learning include the following:

- ♦ They contain presuppositions that are positive, expansive, and self- and other centered.

- ♦ They use qualifying adverbs to promote distinctions between past, present, and future so that assumptions about a positive future can take hold.

- ♦ They use action verbs and clear descriptions to provide or seek distinctions in gradations, levels, qualities.

- ♦ They avoid labeling.

- ♦ They encourage the listener to speak of self, team, or circumstances in an active voice as in soliciting evidence of how we made it happen.

- ♦ There are many genuine questions to check assumptions of self and others.

- ♦ The intent of questions is to obtain information, promote learning, or enhance creativity, and to move toward effective action (Goldberg, 1998).

The following questions (Figure 6.3) were adapted from Goldberg's work in therapeutic settings for use in coaching in schools. The questions on the left result in judgment of self and others, whereas the questions on the right result in learning by self and others. An effective coach will develop trust by shifting the coaching function from assessment for judgment to assessment for learning. As we listen to discussions and explanations from educators, we might hear them answering unasked judgment questions and can help them shift to a focus on learning and possibilities by actually asking a corresponding learning question.

Figure 6.3. Assessment for Learning versus Assessment for Judgment

Stop Using These Questions

Assessment for Judgment Questions

- What's wrong with this data, lesson, student, teacher, team?
- Whose fault is it?
- In what ways are they less or more important, worthy, or significant than we are?
- How can we protect or defend ourselves, colleagues, or school?
- How can we stay in control or avoid going out of control?
- How can we make them see it our way or prove to them we're right?
- Will it make us look good or get approval from ourselves or someone else?
- How can we make them do what we want? How can we get our way?
- How can we get what we want now regardless of how it affects others? How can we win?
- How can we avoid, stop, or control this negative feeling?
- How can we make people change so we don't have to feel this?

Start Using These Questions

Assessment for Learning Questions

- What's right about this data, lesson, student, teacher, team? What's the kindest possible interpretation of him or her or this situation? What are we grateful for in this relationship?
- In what ways are we alike? How could our differences be a contribution to each other? How can we help, serve, support, and empower each other? How can we enjoy sharing information and work appropriately and authentically?
- What are our goals? What are the choices available?
- What can we learn? What categories or areas of ideas are involved? What do we need to know? What's missing that might be important? How else could we think about this?
- What's going on? Are these the facts or simply our opinions? What are our assumptions? Are they valid? Are we avoiding anything? Are we being honest with ourselves?

Start Using These Questions
Assessment for Learning Questions

- Does anything need correcting? How could we do that most effectively? What's the most appropriate way to do this?

- What's our responsibility here, and what are the best ways to fulfill them? How can we contribute to getting this done? How can we handle this most expeditiously, even if we don't feel like it or want to?

- What would be a win-win way to get this done or to resolve this? How can we both win? What are the consequences of our decisions or actions?

- What are we feeling? How can we accept what we're feeling?

- Is this feeling related to the current situation, or is this a throwback to some old situation, person, or feeling? Is this something we can handle by ourselves? Could we use support or help?

- What could we learn from this feeling about ourselves, someone else, or this situation? What's one small thing we can do to help us feel better?

Not only do we need to avoid asking judging questions in coaching situations with teachers, but we need to avoid asking them in our own thinking while leading. Leaders are increasingly overwhelmed and paralyzed as they assess their progress on the myriad of initiatives needed to meet accountability for standards. Judgment questions lead to the blaming of self or others for failures and eventually lead to burn-out of some of the most effective teachers and leaders. Shifting our focus to questions for learning, allows us to approach challenges and changes as opportunities for exploration or discovery not judgment, sentencing, and execution.

Over the last few years we developed a set of coaching questions designed to help teachers and leaders investigate professional practices based on teaching standards closely aligned to the Praxis III test (Dwyer, 1994) and the Danielson framework (Danielson, 1996). The following chart (Figure 6.4) helps the coach understand the level of competence and support needed for professional growth based on national standards through questions in the left hand column and in the right hand column suggests learning questions the coach might pose to promote educator reflection and decisions to use effective teaching practices. We have found that leaders want to ask thoughtful, trusting, reflection questions but often struggle to develop a repertoire of effective questions. We hope these sample questions will jump-start confidence and use of coaching questions.

Figure 6.4. Coaching for Learning Questions

Asking the coaching questions in the right hand column permits teachers to reflect on their teaching in a way that also focuses on improving teaching practices suggested by Danielson (1996) and Dwyer (1994). Listening to the learning reflections permits the coach to answer the coaching reflection questions and plan new conversations or professional development for further improvements in teaching practices.

Teaching Components	Domain A: Organizing Content Knowledge for Student Learning	
	Questions for Coaching Reflections	Questions for Learning Reflections
Becoming familiar with relevant aspects of students' background knowledge and experiences	1. How does the teacher find out about students' background knowledge and experiences? 2. How does the teacher find out about students' foundation for understanding of the content? 3. Is the teacher able to describe why it is important to become familiar with students' background knowledge and experiences? 4. Is the teacher's degree of familiarity with students' background knowledge and experiences adequate in relation to the number of students he or she has?	1. What are some ways you use to discover the students' background knowledge or experience about an upcoming unit? 2. What are some of the reasons that guide your thinking about getting to know your students' background and experiences? 3. How does your awareness of students' background knowledge and experiences impact your student's learning? 4. How do you decide when to seek more information about a student's background or experiences?
Articulating clear learning goals for the lesson that are appropriate for the students	1. Is the teacher able to state learning goals for the current lesson? 2. Does the teacher state the goals in terms of student outcomes, clearly distinguishing outcomes from activities? 3. Does the teacher give a clear rationale for the stated goals? 4. Does the teacher provide different goals for groups or individual students? 5. Does the teacher provide an acceptable explanation of why the differentiated goals are appropriate for groups or individual students?	1. What were all the learning goals for this lesson? 2. How do you move from student outcomes to activities in your lesson planning? 3. Why have you chosen this goal over other goals? 4. How do you decide which goals to use for different groups or individual students? 5. What information do you use when determining to use different goals for different groups of students?

Figure 6.4. Coaching for Learning Questions (continued)

Teaching Components	Questions for Coaching Reflections	Questions for Learning Reflections
Demonstrating an understanding of the connections between the content that was learned previously, the current content, and the content that remains to be learned in the future	1. Can the teacher explain how the content he or she has planned for today connects to what the students have previously learned? 2. Can the teacher explain how the content he or she has planned for today connects to what students will study in the future? 3. To what extent can the teacher explain how today's lesson fits with larger goals of learning in the discipline? 4. Can the teacher explain how the best practices or standards guide selection of content?	1. How does this lesson build on your students' previous learning? 2. How does the learning students engaged in today support learning for future content you have planned? 3. How do you make decisions about which content to emphasize in this content area? 4. When making decisions about which content to teach, what best practices or standards guide your thinking?
Creating or selecting teaching methods, learning activities, and instructional materials or other resources that are appropriate to the students and that are aligned with the goals of	1. Are the methods, activities, materials, and resources selected by the teacher aligned with the goals of the lesson? 2. Are the methods and activities appropriate to the students' developmental levels? Do the materials and activities provide for varied styles of participation? 3. Are the activities, materials, and resources appropriate to the students' developmental levels? Do they reflect the common and unique experiences of different ethnic groups, of males and females, of different economic groups, of groups with exceptionalities? Are the activities and resources appropriate for students of limited English proficiency? 4. If a single activity is used, can the teacher provide a sound explanation of why a single activity is appropriate for all students? 5. Is there evidence that the teacher has considered various methods, activities, and materials, and has considered the advantages and disadvantages of each?	1. How do you make decisions about which materials or resources to use in a lesson? 2. When you are planning a lesson, how do you determine which resources and activities will meet the developmental needs or styles of various students? 3. When you review resources for use in your classroom, what criteria do you use to determine which will be appropriate for the students in your setting? 4. How do you determine when to use a single activity with all of your students? 5. When confronted with many resources or examples from which to choose, how do you determine which resources will best serve the learning needs of your students?

Figure 6.4. Coaching for Learning Questions (continued)

Teaching Components	Questions for Coaching Reflections	Questions for Learning Reflections
Creating or selecting evaluation strategies that are appropriate for students and that are aligned with the goals of the lesson	1. How is the plan for evaluation aligned with the learning goals of the lesson? 2. Is the plan for evaluation sufficiently systematic to provide the teacher with useful information about the extent to which learning goals have been met? 3. Is the evaluation appropriate to the students in the class? What methods are used? How are students of limited English proficiency and students with exceptionalities provided with opportunities to display their knowledge of content? 4. Can the teacher describe how he or she will use the results of the evaluation in planning future instruction?	1. How do you decide which method of evaluation matches the needs of the specific students in your classroom? 2. What are some of the ways you use to determine whether each student understands the content for the lesson? 3. How do you go about deciding which type of assessment is needed to match the learning objective for a lesson? 4. How do student assessments shape your ongoing planning for instruction?

Domain B: Creating an Environment for Student Learning

Teaching Components	Questions for Coaching Reflections	Questions for Learning Reflections
Creating a climate that promotes fairness	1. Is the teacher fair in interactions with students during the observed class period? 2. In what ways does the teacher help students to have access to learning? 3. In what ways does the teacher help the students feel equally valued in the classroom? 4. Are there patterns of either exclusion or over attention in student–teacher interactions? 5. Does the teacher show evidence of stereotyped views of students? 6. Is the teacher inappropriately negative in remarks to students? 7. Do students treat each other fairly? 8. Does the teacher respond appropriately to stereotyped-based, demeaning, or other unfair comments by students?	1. What indicators do you use in the classroom to determine if students feel interactions are fair? 2. How do you assure that each student has access to learning? 3. How do you help each student feel valued in your classroom? 4. When you plan interactions with students, how do work to assure appropriate amounts of attention for each student? 5. What are the strategies you use to focus on each student's unique needs? 6. How do you maintain positive communication patterns in your classroom? 7. How do you assure that students treat each other fairly? 8. When confronted with stereo-typing, demeaning, or unfair comments by students, how do you decide what steps to take?

Figure 6.4. Coaching for Learning Questions (continued)

Teaching Components	Questions for Coaching Reflections	Questions for Learning Reflections
Establishing and maintaining rapport with students	1. Does the teacher attempt to relate positively to students? 2. Does the teacher show concern for the students? 3. Does the teacher tailor personal interactions according to the individual characteristics of students? 4. Do the teacher's attempts to establish rapport take in account students' backgrounds and experiences? 5. Are the teacher's attempts to establish rapport appropriate to the students' developmental levels?	1. What strategies do you use to relate positively to students? 2. What are the things you do that indicate concern for students? 3. How do you develop rapport with different types of students in your classroom? 4. As you develop rapport with students, how do you use information about students' backgrounds and experiences? 5. How do you use students' developmental levels to help you establish appropriate rapport with students?
Communicating challenging learning expectations to each student	1. How does the teacher show, by words, actions, or attitude, that each student is capable of meaningful achievement? 2. In what ways do the students demonstrate a clear understanding of the teacher's expectations for achievement that may have been stated explicitly prior to the observation? 3. Are the learning expectations for students challenging but within their reach?	1. How do you help students know that you think they are capable of achievement? 2. What indications from students do you use to determine that students understand your expectations for achievement? 3. When determining expectations for students, how do you plan on the appropriate amount of challenge for each student?
Establishing and maintaining consistent standards of classroom behavior	1. Are consistent standards of classroom behavior evident? 2. How are standards established? 3. Does the teacher model respectful and appropriate standards of behavior? 4. Do established standards of behavior convey a sense of respect for the students? 5. How are the standards maintained? 6. How does the teacher respond to serious behavior problems? Are her or his responses appropriate? 7. Does the teacher respond to inappropriate behavior consistently and appropriately?	1. How do you decide on a consistent set of standards for behavior? 2. How do you develop a solid understanding and consistent practice of standards for behavior with all of your students? 3. When modeling respectful and appropriate behavior, how do you decide when and how to model the behavior? 4. How do you decide on standards that convey a sense of respect for all students? 5. What strategies do you use that assure that standards are maintained? 6. How do you plan for appropriate responses to behavior problems? 7. What strategies do you use to assure that your responses to inappropriate behavior are consistent and appropriate?

Figure 6.4. Coaching for Learning Questions (continued)

Teaching Components	Questions for Coaching Reflections	Questions for Learning Reflections
Making the physical environment as safe and conducive to learning as possible	1. How much control does the teacher have over the physical environment? 2. Are any safety violations or risks evident? 3. To what extent is there a match between the lesson or activity and the furniture or room configuration? 4. Is the space arranged so that all students, including those with special needs, have access to the lesson? 5. How does the room reflect the learning that takes place there?	1. When examining your physical environment, how do you decide what things you can change? 2. How do you go about assessing your classroom environment for safety violations or risks? 3. When you are planning lessons, how do you plan for the furniture or room configuration needed? 4. What are the decisions you make about assuring physical access to learning by all students? 5. In what ways does your classroom environment reflect the learning that takes place during different units or times of the year?

Domain C: Teaching for Student Learning

Teaching Components	Questions for Coaching Reflections	Questions for Learning Reflections
Making learning goals and instructional procedures clear to students	1. Does the teacher communicate learning goals to the students, either explicitly or implicitly? 2. Are the directions to students for instructional procedures clear? 3. How does the teacher help students of different backgrounds (ethnic groups, language groups, males and females, students with exceptionalities) understand the learning goals of the lesson? 4. How does the teacher help students of different backgrounds (ethnic groups, language groups, males and females, students with exceptionalities) understand the instructional procedures used in the lesson? 5. Are the students able to carry out the instructional procedures?	1. How do you decide which methods to use in communicating your learning goals and instructional procedures? 2. How do you check that your goals and instructions are clear to all your students? 3. How do you use information about the background of students to assure that each group understands the learning goals of the lesson? 4. How do you use information about the background of students to assure that each group understands the instructional procedures used in the lesson? 5. What indicators do you look for to assess whether your students are able to carry out the instructional procedures?

Figure 6.4. Coaching for Learning Questions (continued)

Teaching Components	Questions for Coaching Reflections	Questions for Learning Reflections
Making content comprehensible to students	1. Does the teacher communicate content clearly and accurately? Is this done equitably for females and males, students of different ethnic groups, students of different economic groups, students with exceptionalities, students with limited English proficiency? 2. In lessons that are not teacher-directed, has the teacher structured the learning environment or process in a way that enables students to understand content? 3. Are students generally engaged with the content? 4. Does the lesson as a whole have a coherent structure?	1. How do you use information about students' background and experiences to determine how to engage each learner in the content of the lesson? 2. When you structure a lesson, how do you decide which strategies to use to promote student engagement with the content in the lesson? 3. What are the ways you use to determine whether students are engaged in the learning during a lesson? 4. How do you make decisions about the sequence of content to create a coherent unit?
Encouraging students to extend their thinking	1. Does the teacher recognize and use opportunities to help students extend their thinking? 2. Is the teacher able to use the current content appropriately as a springboard to independent, creative, or critical thinking? 3. Does the teacher challenge students' thinking in ways relevant to their background knowledge and experiences? 4. Does the teacher structure specific learning activities that encourage students to extend their thinking?	1. What are some ways you use to assure that each student extends and advances his or her independent, creative, or critical thinking? 2. When you are planning a unit, how do you determine which questions will connect students to the content to extend their thinking? 3. How do you decide which questions to use with different students during a classroom discussion? 4. When you plan a variety of learning activities in a unit, how do you decide which questions to use to engage students in the activities?
Monitoring students' understanding of content through a variety of means, providing feedback to students to assist learning, and adjusting learning activities as the situation demands	1. Does the teacher monitor students' understanding of the content? Is this done equitably? 2. Does the teacher use a variety of appropriate assessment strategies to monitor understanding of content? Is this done equitably? 3. Does the teacher provide substantive, descriptive feedback to students? Is this done equitably? 4. Does the teacher adjust learning activities as needed? Is the adjustment equitable?	1. What are the various means by which you monitor learning for each student during a lesson? 2. How do you decide what kind of feedback to provide to the class as a whole and to each student? 3. What are the ways in which you involve students in the use of feedback to improve their learning? 4. How do you decide what feedback to provide each student to adjust and improve their future learning?

Figure 6.4. Coaching for Learning Questions (continued)

Teaching Components	Questions for Coaching Reflections	Questions for Learning Reflections
Making content comprehensible to students	1. Does the teacher communicate content clearly and accurately? Is this done equitably for females and males, students of different ethnic groups, students of different economic groups, students with exceptionalities, students with limited English proficiency? 2. In lessons that are not teacher-directed, has the teacher structured the learning environment or process in a way that enables students to understand content? 3. Are students generally engaged with the content? 4. Does the lesson as a whole have a coherent structure?	1. How do you use information about students' background and experiences to determine how to engage each learner in the content of the lesson? 2. When you structure a lesson, how do you decide which strategies to use to promote student engagement with the content in the lesson? 3. What are the ways you use to determine whether students are engaged in the learning during a lesson? 4. How do you make decisions about the sequence of content to create a coherent unit?
Encouraging students to extend their thinking	1. Does the teacher recognize and use opportunities to help students extend their thinking? 2. Is the teacher able to use the current content appropriately as a springboard to independent, creative, or critical thinking? 3. Does the teacher challenge students' thinking in ways relevant to their background knowledge and experiences? 4. Does the teacher structure specific learning activities that encourage students to extend their thinking?	1. What are some ways you use to assure that each student extends and advances his or her independent, creative, or critical thinking? 2. When you are planning a unit, how do you determine which questions will connect students to the content to extend their thinking? 3. How do you decide which questions to use with different students during a classroom discussion? 4. When you plan a variety of learning activities in a unit, how do you decide which questions to use to engage students in the activities?
Monitoring students' understanding of content through a variety of means, providing feedback to students to assist learning, and adjusting learning activities as the situation demands	1. Does the teacher monitor students' understanding of the content? Is this done equitably? 2. Does the teacher use a variety of appropriate assessment strategies to monitor understanding of content? Is this done equitably? 3. Does the teacher provide substantive, descriptive feedback to students? Is this done equitably? 4. Does the teacher adjust learning activities as needed? Is the adjustment equitable?	1. What are the various means by which you monitor learning for each student during a lesson? 2. How do you decide what kind of feedback to provide to the class as a whole and to each student? 3. What are the ways in which you involve students in the use of feedback to improve their learning? 4. How do you decide what feedback to provide each student to adjust and improve their future learning?

Figure 6.4. Coaching for Learning Questions (continued)

Teaching Components	Questions for Coaching Reflections	Questions for Learning Reflections
Using instructional time effectively	1. Is the instruction paced in such a way that students appear to be on task most of the time? 2. Is there evidence of established routines and procedures that help the teacher maximize the time available for instruction? 3. If a noninstructional interruption occurs, is instruction resumed efficiently? 4. Do all students have meaningful work or activities for the entire time?	1. How do you decide how much time to devote to each task to assure that students are on task? 2. How do you plan routines and procedures to maximize the time you have for instruction and student learning? 3. What strategies do you use to promptly resume instruction when noninstructional interruptions occur? 4. What strategies do you use to assure that learning is happening throughout the instructional time?

Domain D: Teacher Professionalism

Teaching Components	Questions for Coaching Reflections	Questions for Learning Reflections
Reflecting on the extent to which the learning goals were met	1. What judgments does the teacher make about the extent to which the goals were met? Are these judgments accurate? 2. How does the teacher support her or his judgment? 3. What explanation does the teacher give for deviations from the instructional plan? 4. How does the teacher analyze the effectiveness of her or his teaching strategies? 5. How does the teacher articulate ways in which insights gained from this lesson could be used to improve future instruction?	1. How do you determine whether your goals were met? 2. What are some of the indications that you met your goal? 3. What criteria do you use when you decide to change your instructional plan? 4. When you think about your lesson, what criteria do you use to decide whether the strategies you used were effective or not? 5. How will you use insights you gained from this lesson to improve future instruction?
Demonstrating a sense of efficacy	1. In what ways does the teacher convey a sense of efficacy with respect to students' learning? 2. What specific actions does the teacher suggest for working with individual students who are not meeting the learning goals?	1. What skills or experiences do you think you can use in the future to increase student learning? 2. When students are not meeting the learning goals, how do you determine which actions to take?

Figure 6.4. Coaching for Learning Questions (continued)

Teaching Components	Questions for Coaching Reflections	Questions for Learning Reflections
Building professional relationships with colleagues to share teaching insights and to coordinate learning activities for students	1. Does the teacher identify colleagues within the school who can provide instructional help that is relevant to the observed lesson or to students in the class? 2. If appropriate, does the teacher identify colleagues whose participation is either necessary or helpful in coordinating learning activities for students? 3. Does the teacher consult with colleagues on matters related to learning and instruction or other professional matters? 4. In what ways does the teacher collaborate with colleagues outside his or her classroom to coordinate learning activities or address other teaching concerns?	1. When you need help to improve your instruction, how do you identify which colleagues can provide the best assistance? 2. How do you go about deciding when to coordinate learning activities with other colleagues? 3. On what types of matters do you consult with other colleagues? 4. What are the ways in which you invite collaboration with your colleagues?
Communicating with parents or guardians about students	1. Does the teacher demonstrate knowledge of how he or she could communicate with parents or guardians? 2. Does the teacher communicate appropriately with parents or guardians in ways that are suitable for his or her teaching situation? 3. Does the communication result in increased understanding of how student learning can be increased?	1. What are the means by which you typically communicate with families? 2. How do you go about finding out how families prefer to receive information and communication about their students? 3. How do your communications with families increase your understanding about how to increase student learning?

Coaching questions were adapted from: Dwyer, C. A. (1994). *Praxis III: Classroom Performance Assessments Assessment Criteria*. Princeton, NJ: Educational Testing Service.

Many of the questions in the coaching for learning chart (see Figure 6.4) can be used by us, as leaders, to self-reflect on our own practices. If coaching is such an important tool in our change arsenal, we should spend time coaching one another and should also be open to coaching educators and leaders alike. Specific coaching questions for leaders based on national leadership standards have yet to be developed. We see value in the development of such a set of coaching questions, and we hope others will join us in this important work. In the meantime, we encourage leaders to use the coaching for learning questions (see Figure 6.4) with other leaders in leadership PLCs.

What are Some Strategies or Approaches to Coaching We Can Use in Schools?

There are a variety of coaching approaches that can be used from self-coaching to peer coaching, to formal observations, to portfolio documents. At the heart of coaching is the desire to help the teacher or leader become more aware of what they know and can do. This may result in a change in behavior or beliefs or just confirm and extend effective practices and beliefs. Let's examine the range of coaching approaches that might be possible.

Teachers can coach themselves through self-reflection or journaling. One principal we know purchased spiral notebooks for each faculty member when he entered a new school and distributed them at the first faculty meeting. He systematically posed questions during faculty meetings and then used the meeting time for the teachers to self-reflect and journal. He expected that they would continue to do so outside of the faculty meeting. Teachers in a year-long learning community (Foord, 2004) were required to self-reflect and share evidence of how they were meeting the teaching standards in Danielson's framework (1996) with members in their PLC.

School leaders and teachers can use one-on-one observations and the traditional pre-, during, and post-observation process to focus attention on one or more coaching questions. Some districts provide release time for special coaches (usually teachers) to do this work. Peer coaching can be a great way to encourage teacher-to-teacher coaching. Observations can be conducted by matching up two teachers with preparation periods that are different to avoid the use of substitute teachers. If teachers have the same preparation period, the peer coaching can be scheduled and professional development funds can pay for rotating substitute teachers. Finally, the use of video-taped lessons permits the teacher, peer coach, or administrator to conduct a joint observations where all parties see and analyze the teaching together. National Board Certified teachers (NBPTS, 1989) rely heavily on video self-analysis to improve and document teacher proficiency.

In one district in which we worked, teachers were trained to use the coaching for learning questions (see Figure 6.4) as part of a peer coaching process. The district narrowed the focus of professional growth to eight components on the list. During the year, each teacher received two observations from their colleagues in their PLC. Two teachers from the PLC observe a third colleague, determined one coaching for learning question (see Figure 6.4) they believed would help their colleague grow, and conducted a short coaching session using that question. They posed the learning question, and all three participants recorded their reflections based on the reflections of the teacher being coached. All participants, observers and observed, gained from this learning experience through self-reflection. With two teachers coaching, trust and learning were enhanced because they were required to agree on one trust-building question, a process that also prioritized and refined the focus for improving teaching practices in line with the PLCs goals. This also permitted the coaching conference to be short, focused, and productive. The following forms (Figures 6.5 and 6.6) were used to focus the observation on goals and teaching practices and to record insights from the conference. These forms became part of the teachers' portfolios used to document work in PLCs. The portfolios were used as part of a pay for performance system that was partially based on their contribution to one another's learning.

Figure 6.5. Peer Coaching Pre-Observation Form

Date of preconference: _____

Date and time of observation: _____

Faculty member who will be observed and teaching area:

_____

PLC goal and/or sub-goal being addressed:

What would you like us to look for in our observation today?

What domains or specific teaching practices do you want us to focus on?

Peer coaches observing (no more than 2):

1. _____

_____

2. _____

_____

Figure 6.6. Peer Observation Feedback Form

Teacher Observed _____ Date _____

Peer Observers _____

_____

Component	Assessment for Learning Question	Teacher Reflections
Demonstrating knowledge of content		
Demonstrating knowledge of students		
Demonstrating knowledge of resources		
Assessing student learning		
Using questioning and discussion techniques		
Engaging students in learning		
Providing feedback to students		
Reflection on teaching		
Other feedback requested? (specify)		

The classroom walk-throughs (Downey, Steffy, English, & Frase, 2004) that were mentioned by Teresa in the chapter vignette permit principals and teachers to observe several classes in a short amount of time; taking from 3 to 30 minutes to gather observations about specific strategies or practices that are valued by the observers. Some principals we know gather information from five observations before they craft a focusing question for coaching, although others may send an e-mail to each teacher after each observation. Some use the observations to help them determine which single question should be asked of the whole faculty at the next faculty meeting. A leader could leave a question with a teacher at the end of the walk-through or e-mail a question to the teacher. The leader could combine this with a professional journal for each teacher in which they could record their reflections on these coaching questions. To involve teachers in the process, the leader might ask teachers to pose a learning question that they wish to discuss with the leader following the walk-through. This helps the teacher learn and internalize the coaching for learning questions (see Figure 6.4) so that they become self-directed assessors of their own professional growth while eliciting input and feedback from the leader. In one district, a large pool of substitute teachers was used to release all the teachers in one building to conduct walk-throughs in another building to increase the examples of teaching that were observed and the depth of reflection that faculty experienced in both buildings.

When coaching questions are used in faculty meetings, the leader should ask a single question that would impact the practices of all teachers. To engage all in learning, require a silent "all write" period followed by a paired sharing. Another option is to have small group PLCs discuss the question and share out with other PLC groups.

Video study can be used for coaching in PLCs. One teacher in the PLC shares his or her own video segment with the other PLC members, and the group practices selecting a coaching question. Once the group selects and poses a question, both the individual teacher and the PLC members reflect in private about the evidence and/or strategies they observed or used in the lesson. The individual teacher shares his or her reflections followed by supportive observations from the PLC members. Once PLC groups have had some practice in this type of coaching, they may be asked to model one segment for the entire faculty. In fact, when teaching teachers or leaders how to use this approach, we have found that using video clips from outside vendors works well because the person in the video is a stranger, and any missteps teachers and leaders make during initial practice will not harm their own PLC relationships.

Coaching for increased student achievement is supported through the use of student work protocols. Teachers or leaders bring samples of student work and then work in PLCs to examine the work for strengths and areas of improvement. Suggestions for new approaches to teaching surface that address the needs of the specific students whose work is examined, but all teachers in the PLC gain understanding about how changes in practices might support student achievement through this process. The Looking at Student Work organization online has several student work protocols that can be used to support this process (http://www.lasw.org). If PLC meetings are short, and formal protocols take too much time to complete, student work samples can also be analyzed from the perspective of one of the questions from the coaching for learning questions (see Figure 6.4).

Some districts require educators to maintain portfolios with reflections and samples of evidence demonstrating growth in selected teaching standards or practices. The process of keeping a portfolio assures that self-coaching will occur, but it also encourages PLC discussions about what should be in the portfolio and how to document reflections. This supports PLC growth in communication, interdependence, group processing, and individual and group accountability. The portfolio is the individual accountability product that demonstrates the strength of each educator and the PLC group. We encourage developing some means by which coaching questions result in documentation either by the educator or PLC group, preferably both. The following form (Figure 6.7) was developed in one district to assure collection and reflection based on multiple forms of evidence to document specific competencies in educator portfolios.

Figure 6.7. Portfolio Evidence File

Name _____   Building/Grade/Subject _____

This chart encourages teachers to select multiple sources of evidence to support self-assessment on each target competency. They can use the chart to list sources of evidence for each competency and for each type of evidence the district deems important. The evidence tags below permit teachers to describe the evidence in more detail.

Target Competencies	Goal Achievement Evidence	Formal and Informal Observations and Coaching Feedback	Student Work Samples with Teacher Reflection	Aligned Curriculum and Assessment Designs	Parent Communication
1.					
2.					
3.					
4.					
5.					

Evidence Tags—These are used to collect evidence purposefully during the reflection period. Teachers are asked to tag work as the year progresses with written reflections. The types of evidence are recorded in the grid above to assure that multiple evidence sources.

What Does the Evidence Show?	How Does the Evidence Show This?	What Level of Competency Does the Evidence Demonstrate and Why?
☐ Goal achievement ☐ Observations and feedback ☐ Student work and reflection ☐ Aligned curriculum & assessment ☐ Parent Communication		

Finally, coaching questions can reinforce awareness and movement through the change cycle process. Learning community meetings hold greater value to participants when conversations stay focused throughout the change process. Discussions need to progress through assessing needs, addressing new learning, moving to application, and finally reflecting on results and future implications. If conversations stagnate on assessing needs, educators and leaders become despondent because they are not moving forward to meet these perceived needs. In one district, so many years were spent finding and organizing the right assessment data that teachers and building leaders lost confidence in the ability of district leaders to help them turn around their failing scores. Educators and leaders really do want to learn and make a difference. We suggest the following general questions (Figure 6.8) to focus discussions and coaching on the four stages in the change cycle.

Figure 6.8. Coaching Questions for the Change Cycle

Evaluating

Reflect to surface learning:

What ideas came to you as you reflected on your application of new learning?

What is it that you saw students or teachers doing to indicate to you that the application was successful?

What is it that you did to cause this?

What was it about the teaching strategy that produced the outcomes?

Collaborate with others to extend learning:

Based on your analysis, what was the impact on students and teachers?

What next steps will you take?

How do we improve understanding, involvement, use, and assessment of the new learning?

How has this process of reflecting shaped your thinking?

Understanding

Awareness of learning needs:

How do various forms of data (demographics, achievement, perceptions, and school process) inform your understanding of the learning need?

How does your awareness of student and teacher background knowledge and experiences impact your understanding of the needs identified?

How does your awareness translate into stories, beliefs, and expectations for learning?

Information about self, students, school, community:

What are some ways you use to discover the needs of your students, teachers, leaders, or community?

How do you decide when to seek more information?

Operationalizing

Practice learning with assistance:

How does the format of the experience help participants to apply the intended knowledge and skills?

How do participants assist one another in learning to apply the intended knowledge and skills?

Apply to a real setting:

How do participants apply the new knowledge and skills?

How does application of the new learning match your expectations for your ability to use the new learning?

How does your assessment of your application match the results you expected?

Internalizing

Deciding what to learn:

What information do you use when determining which learning goals will be the focus for different groups of teachers?

Why have you chosen this goal over other goals?

Effective learning:

How does the format of the experience help participants to acquire the intended knowledge and skills?

What are some of the ways you use to determine whether each teacher understands the new learning?

Resources for learning:

How do you make decisions about which materials or resources to use while learning?

How do you determine which resources and activities will meet the developmental needs or styles of various teachers?

Take a moment to review each of the innovation maps, looking at implementation level 2 and level 3. How can we use the coaching principles and questions discussed in this chapter to lead changes in our PLC implementation? What principles, practices, and questions will help us to promote additional changes? How can we incorporate more coaching into our leadership practices? How can we help teacher leaders become more adept at coaching? Strengthening teacher and leader skills in coaching through PLCs will promote change in teaching practices and will improve student learning.

Post Vignette

Teresa and the principals in her PLC became more familiar with the Danielson framework and decided to narrow the focus of their observations and coaching for tenured teachers to three key components that also aligned to their building goals. In a faculty meeting, Teresa introduced her teachers to the three key components and the assessment for learning questions they might ask themselves and each other during discussions in their PLCs. She invited PLCs to conduct discussions about the evidence they had or needed to demonstrate proficiency in each component. Teresa conducted walk-throughs to gather evidence and used coaching questions in faculty meetings to increase teacher awareness, reflection, and learning. She began to collect observation notes on index cards and developed a spreadsheet to document the coaching questions she used with each teacher to avoid using the same question over and over again with one teacher.

During an observation of a veteran teacher, she became quite concerned about the practices she observed. She selected several coaching questions and discussed the best approach to coaching this teacher with her principal PLC. The coaching session began with some tension and fear, but concluded with the teacher developing ideas for changes that he could implement to improve student learning. Teresa used the coaching for learning in the change cycle to assess her own progress in supporting PLC development and used the coaching for learning questions to monitor and document her role as an instructional leader. She organized her evidence of progress and the principals in her PLC regularly shared their evidence to determine how to move forward. The principals e-mailed one another reflecting on their selection of coaching questions and how the questions impacted teacher beliefs and practices. This helped them become more fluid and confident in their coaching.

Vignette Analysis

Teresa has greatly expanded her coaching skills and those of her faculty and in doing so will accelerate the implementation of PLCs. She wisely narrowed the focus of teacher professional growth to three components. She distributed the coaching to her teachers by involving them in using the assessment for learning questions in faculty meetings and PLCs. This also expanded trust for the process through making the questions transparent.

Teresa found a way to maintain records of her observations and the coaching questions she used and has actively involved the principals in her own PLC in collaborating to improve their use of walk-throughs and coaching questions. In addition, she has used the questions to assess her own leadership and document progress in implementing PLCs. She has developed individual accountability systems and shares her coaching and documentation with principals in her PLC to increase the group's success. Teresa is definitely on level 2 in her use of coaching to improve teacher learning. We would encourage her to expand her coaching skills by using them to observe PLC meetings and focus attention on development of inter-personal skills, group processing, and teacher's accountability for their work. Just as she has been developing documentation of her progress, she might now monitor and coach teachers as they document their work in PLCs.

Reflecting Forward

◆ At what level of implementation in coaching are teachers and leaders?

◆ What evidence do you have that documents this level of implementation for teachers and leaders?

◆ What evidence would you need to move to the next level of implementation?

◆ What new learning and resources (physical and human) would you need to increase coaching using effective questions?

◆ What practices would you need to use to move to the next level of implementation?

◆ What evidence would you collect and reflect on to assess progress toward more effective coaching?

◆ Who will you involve when reflecting on your new learning about effective questioning and coaching?

◆ With whom will you collaborate to improve the learning or implement the new learning across your school and/or district?

You may find the following format (Figure 6.9) helpful as you process the guiding questions.

Figure 6.9. Guiding Questions Process Form

Where are we, and what evidence do we have of our current level of implementation?	Where do we want to be, and what evidence do we need to move to the next level of implementation?

7

Built to Last

Vignette 7

The conversation Teresa had with her superintendent caused some anxiety. School board members had heard grumbling from parents upset about the "early release time" used for PLCs. The parents were not seeing enough results and had requested a full report about PLC progress. Teresa thought, "What timing." She was finally seeing changes in teachers' assumptions about teaching and learning. Teachers were making changes in their practices based on research and on analysis of student work. They had gained enough interpersonal skills and group processing skills to effectively interact and to hold each other accountable for student growth as well as their own growth. Teresa was hearing professional conversations as she moved about the building. Teachers were getting the idea that PLCs were a way of life—one that allowed them to truly engage in practices that improved learning for all students. How had this powerful realization not been extended to include parents? Teresa would turn to her principal PLC and her leadership team for help with the report.

Guiding Questions

- How can we continue to improve PLCs?
- How can we sustain PLCs?

Professional learning communities honor our profession by supporting teacher work in a collaborative, supportive environment intent on improving student and teacher learning. We create such an environment by balancing the support of current teacher work with an expectation for continuous improvement. We create a culture that respects the hard work of teaching by making PLCs a routine practice of the profession.

Leaders committed to improving PLCs are aware of the level of intensity needed to make effective PLCs a reality; they know they cannot leave things to chance and that the concept of PLCs extends well beyond structuring PLC meetings. Making PLCs a part of the culture involves skilled internal and external communications; risk taking; and the development of self analysis, questioning, and reflection. As school leaders we not only need to encourage such efforts; we must expect and nurture them. The sustainability of PLCs is not a casual or lucky occurrence. It involves leadership that demonstrates patience, careful planning, modeling and hard work. The story of this hard work must be documented and shared to assure that the total culture—students, staff, leaders, parents, and community—understands their roles and responsibilities in sustaining the culture of caring and achievement.

How Can We Continue to Improve Professional Learning Communities?

In conjunction with providing strong leadership, we can continue to improve PLCs by adhering to the purposes of PLCs and documenting improvements that have been made to achieve those purposes. In Chapter 1 we shared four purposes for PLCs: to promote student learning, promote adult learning, professionalize teacher practice, and change education. As we face the interruptions, challenges, and ambiguity that accompany our day-to-day activities, it becomes important to keep the four purposes clear in our minds. We share a brief overview of the purposes to reemphasize their importance with improving teaching and learning.

Promote Student Learning

We need to continually evaluate individual and collective assumptions about student learning. Assumptions that strengthen PLC implementation include the following:

- Effective student learning requires that every teacher is an effective professional who actively seeks ways to improve his or here practice. Individual teachers working in PLCs must bear the responsibility for changing practices to meet the needs of each student.
- Data (and not just test data) must be used by PLCs to address individual students' readiness, interest, and learning styles.

- Curriculum, instruction, and assessment must be differentiated in the regular classroom. Additional support systems and interventions should be available when demonstrated differentiation efforts have not met a student's needs.

- Learning must be rigorous, relevant, and supportive of healthy relationships among students, teachers, and the community at large.

- Motivation to learn must be supported through clear targets and specific frequent feedback.

Promote Adult Learning

We need to continually evaluate how well we are adhering to adult learning principles. Practices that strengthen PLC implementation include:

- Adults should measure their learning against professional standards (Danielson, 1996; Foord, 2004). The relevance of their learning should be visible in improvements in their own practice and the achievement of their students. Adults, just like children, need clear and stable targets to motivate learning and develop their sense of self and collective efficacy (Stiggins et al., 2006).

- Adults need to construct their learning in social settings and reflect on the impact of their learning to solve real problems or concerns that they have chosen. Adults learn best when their efforts are self-directed and when they negotiate the meaning of their learning through social transactions (Merriam et al., 2007).

- Significant changes in practice result from a cycle of learning that develops understanding for the need for change, allows personalization of commitment and learning, encourages practice with reflection on results, and promotes collaboration to improve results (Foord, 2004; Hall & Hord, 2001).

Professionalize Teaching Practice

We need to continually evaluate how well we are adhering to professional practices. Reasons for professionalizing the practice that strengthen PLC implementation include:

- *Teachers are professionals not technicians.* A technically proficient teacher lacks the energy, creativity, and determination to reach each child. We want teachers who plan and implement rich, developmentally appropriate curriculum in ways that are instructionally responsive to the diverse students in their classrooms. We want teachers who connect to other professionals, to parents, and to the community in ways that promote healthy, collaborative relationships that support student learning. We want teachers who are passionate about their profession and who clearly demonstrate that they care about their students.

- *Teachers deserve professional learning and growth.* We dream of individual professional growth plans tied to each teacher's needs to increase student achievement. We imagine teacher managed growth plans that document professional development, practice, and reflection with other professionals on a daily basis. Just as we hope for differentiated instruction for our students we hope for differentiated learning for our teachers. We want job-embedded learning where adults enthusiastically self-direct their professional practices with each other in response to real student needs.

- *Positive interdependence distributes the effort and workload.* We want teachers who understand how issues affect us as a whole and initiate important work to serve our children, families, school, and broader community. We cannot lead everything and need to develop leaders among our teachers whom we and others can follow.

- *Collective strength and efficacy leads to a successful, learning organization.* We want and need teachers who learn and grow together to produce synergistic, collective knowledge and responsibility to address student learning and organizational problems. We want to sustain the system because the organization remembers and responds, not just individual teachers. If one person leaves, school success will continue.

Change Education

We need to continually evaluate how well we are adhering to change principles that affect educational change. Principles that strengthen PLC implementation include:

- Changes in practice lead to changes in beliefs (Foord, 2004; Fullan, 1995; Pfeffer & Sutton, 2000) not the other way around. Attempting to persuade teachers to align their practices to district beliefs such as mission, vision, or goals will not promote changes in practice if those beliefs are not already held by the teachers.

- Change comes when teachers share a common concern and commit to changes because of a common purpose. This common purpose is not one imposed externally but one that is developed through deep discussion and reflection on commonly held values and visible results from changes in practice.

♦ Change in practice requires clear targets for effective professional practices and specific, frequent feedback on proficiency (Danielson, 1996; NBPTS, 1989; Stiggins et al., 2006).

♦ Changes in practice are the result of time spent in a cycle of implementation that honors the four stages of change: Understanding, personalization, operationalization, and evaluation (Foord, 2004; Hall & Hord, 2001).

♦ Effective change can be enhanced by monitoring the level of use of new practices and supporting higher levels of implementation (Hall & Hord, 2001).

♦ Effective leaders will ask themselves how changes in PLCs have addressed these four major purposes to document and share the successes that will sustain the culture or alter the course for improvements in practices.

How Can We Sustain Professional Learning Communities?

Sustainability is the ultimate goal. Until we reach the point where PLCs are a natural and expected part of the culture, we cannot relax. And even when PLCs become a part of the culture, we will need to attend to sustainability. We sustain PLCs by monitoring the effectiveness of implementation. Continual assessment is essential. In our work, we have found the following tools and techniques useful to sustain PLCs.

Use Innovation Maps to Measure and Monitor Implementation

The innovation maps are a resource that can be used to measure and monitor progress with PLC implementation. Leaders can use them to assess the level of implementation of faculty and self; teachers can use them as a self-assessment instrument or as a group assessment within their small PLC; and the whole faculty can use them as a building level assessment.

The innovation maps focus on the academic and the relational practices of PLC implementation. The first three maps address the "what" of PLCs; the next four maps address the "how" of PLCs. One final innovation map is introduced later in this chapter to monitor the "big picture" or sustainability of PLCs. The innovation maps provide a continuous assessment process to measure and guide individual and group progress.

Monitor Movement in the Change Cycle

The process of using innovation maps can, in turn, support the change process. Individuals or groups can move through the change cycle to determine how they are doing with any of the innovation map elements: student learning and growth, professional learning and growth, PLC development, interdependence, interpersonal interactions, group processing, individual and/or group accountability, and sustainability.

If the change cycle is used as a common language to share practices by an individual or a group, the learning can be better understood by other individuals, other PLC groups or the entire faculty. We can and should encourage this level of sharing if we hope to institutionalize the practices and skills developed through PLCs. It should become common practice for us to continually reflect on such questions as "What do I know about my students, and what are the consequences for these students from the changes we are making?" and "What are the consequences (relational and academic) for me and others from working together as a PLC team?"

As leaders we need to expect questioning and reflection from all faculty. Through leadership, modeling, and encouragement, we can establish a culture where questioning, reflection,

> There is an abundance of knowledge and skill within every building that is either underused or untapped.

and collaboration become as second nature for all teachers as classroom procedures become for experienced teachers. We should expect our teachers to be asking questions of colleagues, asking questions about one another's practices, making connections between teams and faculty, making applications of new learning to other subjects and disciplines, and asking "Where do we go next?" and "What does this mean for us?"

Our responsibility is to "systemize" the sharing. There is an abundance of knowledge and skill within every building that is either under used or untapped. At times, we are simply unaware of each others' knowledge and skill, or we lack the time to share. We can sustain teacher growth by intentionally developing a culture and a system that allows for the knowledge and skill levels of our teachers to be respected and shared. We, as leaders, must create an atmosphere where teachers feel comfortable to take risks with their teaching, to share their work with others and to openly ask questions that allow them to reflect on their effectiveness. If we consistently repeat the following reflection questions: "What do we want?"; "What are we doing and how is it working?"; and "What may help us?" we can create a nonthreatening environment that allows teachers to internalize the process of sharing and collective responsibility to inquiry.

Such a process allows teachers to share what they are working on, to reflect on how has it affected students; and to openly discuss approaches that haven't worked, why they haven't worked, and what we are going to do about it. The process can effectively expand across grade levels, schools, and systems. For instance, we witnessed an incident where an elementary teacher helped a group of secondary math instructors explore the use of graphic organizers as an effective tool for organizing student thinking.

Ongoing assessment through the use of the change cycle can also transform the way teachers think and operate. It can become a habit for them to identify and share evidence on a continuous basis as they cycle through the quadrants of the change cycle. For instance, in the first quadrant (understanding), evidence collected and analyzed can include data profiles (achievement, demographics, perceptions, and processes), teacher efficacy surveys, observations of teaching, student work, group processing forms, teacher and group reflections. In the second quadrant (internalizing), evidence could include surveys of the level of use of research-based strategies, assessment of the resource budget, and measures of teacher proficiency (content, pedagogy, interpersonal or group processing skills). During new learning, formative assessments of the learning might include lesson plans, discussions, or group work products. In the third quadrant (practice), evidence could be collected and analyzed through walk-throughs, conversations, student work protocols, and team processing reports on how the group functions; and finally, in the fourth quadrant (evaluation), evidence could include interpersonal surveys, self-observations by teams, team-coaching questions, and individual and team notebooks that capture impact and reflections. Using multiple sources of evidence provides faculty with a data set with which to process and refocus on how well they are meeting student needs and their own professional growth needs. The refocusing process allows for "commitment input" from teachers—thus keeping them involved. It is the leader's responsibility to garner and share a collective data set of the evidence used in each quadrant so teachers can move into the next cycle of learning.

Analyze Levels of Use of New Initiatives

Another tool available to monitor the continuous improvement of PLCs is Hall and Hord's (2001) level of use protocol (Figure 7.1). The protocol was designed to measure the degree of implementation of innovations. We modified the levels of use protocol to categorize data about changes and the change processes. As school leaders we can use the levels of use to evaluate how we are progressing with PLC implementation. We can also use the levels of use to determine what kind of support or guidance is needed to increase the level of implementation.

Figure 7.1. Hall and Hord's Modified Levels of Use

Levels of Change	Description of Level
0	No use or change, no knowledge or involvement in changes
1	**Orientation**—recently acquired or is acquiring information about innovation or change
2	**Preparation**—preparing for first use of innovation or change
3	**Mechanical**—short-term, day-to-day innovation and/or change with little reflection, superficial use, or change
4A	**Routine**—Use and/or change is stabilized. Few, if any, ongoing changes are being made.
4B	**Refinement**—User varies the use and/or change to increase impact on students. Variation is based on knowledge of consequences for students.
5	**Integration**—User combines own efforts to change with related activities of colleagues to achieve a collective impact on students.
6	**Renewal**—User reevaluates the quality of changes, seeks major modifications or alternatives to increase impact on students, examines new developments in the field, and explores new goals for self and system.

Leaders can ask the following questions to determine the level of use of the innovations.

♦ Are there changes in beliefs and practices about effective teaching? (This helps clarify and organize understanding about the content for change.)

♦ Are there plans to change in the future? Have you set a date? (This helps us understand the level of preparation toward change.)

♦ Are you seeking more information about the change? (This helps us understand their orientation toward the change. It also helps us understand whether changes are mechanical and routine or have moved on to be refined through reflection and new knowledge.)

♦ What kind of changes in beliefs or practices are happening? (This gets at the specific content and evidence of changes.)

♦ What led to these changes? (This question helps us understanding the process or reasons for change.)

♦ Are you coordinating your use of the innovation with other users, including others not in your original group of users? Have you shared or are you planning to share changes or modifications outside of the learning community? (These questions surface evidence of integrating changes and the degree of integration with others.)

♦ Are you planning or exploring major modifications or changes in the innovations? (This question helps us understand how the change is being extended or adapted for renewal.)

If we know the level of use teachers are experiencing, we can more effectively document change in the innovation maps and also gauge our coaching questions and support for transitions to higher levels of innovation.

Aligning Policies, Practices, and Infrastructures

Schools usually have good intentions when they establish policies, practices, and infrastructures. At times, however, we may maintain a policy or practice more out of habit or efficiency than out of effectiveness or support for student learning. Careful examination of policies, practices, and infrastructures may uncover procedures that hinder teaching efforts and student learning. In effective PLCs, teachers will identify and request procedural changes: These can be as minimal as a change in hallway monitoring or as significant as a complete schedule change.

As we develop and realign policies and practices that affect student and adult learning, we also monitor and assess the effectiveness of the changes. Important changes in practice can be erased if they remain informal; the changes can be lost when even one person leaves a school, but when the changes are systematically recorded as the policies and practices, they become etched in our collective memories as the "story" of our organization—a "story" that is shared with new members as an expectation for our culture (Hargreaves, 1994).

The following form (Figure 7.2), based on the National Staff Development Council (NSDC) *Standards for Staff Development* (2001), demonstrates how a school can monitor and assess changes to policy and practice that support PLC implementation. The sample stems from use of the form in a school district that had implemented PLCs in conjunction with a state-level grant.

Figure 7.2. Sample—PLC Sustainability Self-Assessment: Institutionalization of Policy, Practice, and Capacity and Infrastructure

Components of Institutionalization	Policy	Practice	Capacity/Infrastructure
Vision and leadership	The school board incorporated the implementation of PLCs into the district's strategic plan with innovation maps and the change cycle as identified assessment instruments.	School leaders have adopted the use of innovation maps to evaluate the effectiveness of PLC implementation in their buildings.	Innovation maps are used by PLC groups to assess progress with PLC goals.
Curriculum	District policies involving curriculum are being revised to support district standards.	PLC groups regularly compare curriculum to district standards and assessments.	As the curriculum is reviewed during the annual cycle, the district curriculum coordinator guides the curriculum committee to review and imbed curriculum suggestions from PLC groups.
Professional development	The district level professional development committee received school board support for the implementation of the change cycle as a district level assessment instrument.	Each building has a teacher leader who serves as a site facilitator of the change cycle.	The district level professional development committee analyzes building level implementation of the change cycle at monthly meetings.
Partnership and community	The district establishes a formal partnership with the local university to collaboratively work toward the institutionalization of PLCs.	A university liaison meets with the building leadership team once a month.	The university liaison collaborates with the building leadership team to implement the continuous collection, analysis, and communication of PLC work.
Continuous improvement	The district adopts policy that aligns continuous improvement plans to district level PLC beliefs, expectations and actions.	Continuous improvement plans are developed based on identified student and teacher needs.	Buildings use the continuous improvement plans for decision-making focused on student and professional growth.

Professional Learning Community Sustainability Self-Assessment:
Institutionalization of Policy, Practice, and Capacity/Infrastructure

Components of Institutionalization	Policy	Practice	Capacity/Infrastructure
Vision and leadership			
Curriculum			
Professional development			
Partnership and community			
Continuous improvement			

As you reflect on your current level of implementation of PLCs, which policies, practices, and infrastructures are visible as sustainable commitments?

Support Teacher Leadership and Distributed Leadership

Teacher leadership and distributed leadership also support the sustainability of PLCs. Teacher leaders, according to Danielson (2006) perform the following tasks: (a) use evidence and data in decision making, (b) recognize opportunity and take initiative, (c) mobilize people around a common purpose, (d) marshal resources and take action, (e) monitor progress and adjust the approach as conditions change, (f) sustain the commitment of others and anticipate negativity, and (g) contribute to the learning organization. Teacher leaders possess a deep commitment to student learning; are optimistic and enthusiastic, open minded and humble, courageous and willing to take risks, confident and decisive, tolerate ambiguity, are creative and flexible, persevere, and are willing to work hard. By developing teacher leaders with these characteristics, we, as school leaders, can confidently distribute the responsibility for the work of PLCs and ensure their sustainability. The most valuable resource in any school rests with individual and collective teaching and leading capabilities. Developing these capabilities is a key priority to sustaining high functioning schools.

Distributive leadership, the "sharing of leadership by two or more individuals" (www.e-lead.org), has become widespread as schools build leadership capacity. Leverett (2002) notes, "Professional learning communities and high-performance organizations support the wisdom of distributing leadership to achieve organizational goals" (p. 2). Skillful school leaders understand the value of teacher leadership and distribute leadership responsibilities among teachers and other employees. They also make certain that the teachers have the necessary knowledge and skills as well as the necessary support to ensure success in their new roles. Distributed leadership enables teachers to develop and use their talents through experiences as members or chairs of school improvement committees, trainers, coaches, mentors, and members of peer-review panels. Many of the schools with whom we work regularly involve teacher leadership teams in reviewing documentation from building PLCs to determine professional development and resource needs. These teams serve as crucial resources when determining changes in policies, practices, and timelines. Some schools are designating which members of their staff will lead them in data analysis, literacy strategies, culturally responsive strategies, and formative assessment development to capitalize on these teacher leaders' talents and distribute responsibilities.

Strengthen Efficacy and Celebrate Successes

In addition to supporting teacher leadership and distributive leadership, school leaders are also responsible for encouraging teachers to take risks and to be innovative with their teaching. The challenge is tricky as leaders work to create a balance between expecting the consistent implementation of standards, practices and policies while also encouraging the kind of risk-taking and innovation that allows the profession to grow in its understanding and implementation of effective teaching. Leaders can establish a balance by strengthening individual and collective efficacy toward trying new practices and techniques and by celebrating the successes that occur from taking such risks. Of key importance in celebrating "success" are those that support student and teacher growth. To support implementation of PLC innovations there should be ample opportunities to celebrate such things as growth in skills (including interpersonal and group skills), professionalism, collective efficacy, and team recognition. Celebrations of effective processes are just as important in reinforcing sustainable innovations as celebrations of student results. Efficacy and success can also be acknowledged through specific actions such as securing funding for team performance. For instance, with a number of alternative pay proposals surfacing in education, school leaders can develop proposals that recognize and honor the collaborative, effective results of teacher growth and processes in PLC work in addition to results from student achievement. In one school, teachers believed they had become much better teachers and highly valued their PLCs. They attributed this to the fact that more emphasis in their alternative pay system was placed on how well teachers collaborated, coached, and reflected with one another than on specific student achievement gains.

According to NSDC, skillful leaders "ensure an equitable distribution of resources to accomplish district goals and continuously improve the school or district's work through the ongoing evaluation of staff development's effectiveness in achieving student learning goals. They make certain that employee contracts, annual calendars, and daily schedules provide adequate time for learning and collaboration as part of the workday. In addition, they align district incentive systems with demonstrated knowledge and skill and improvements in student learning rather than seat-time arrangements such as courses completed or continuing education units earned" (www.nsdc.org/standards/).

> Celebrations of effective processes are just as important in reinforcing sustainable innovations as celebrations of student results.

Innovation Map Eight—Sustaining Professional Learning Communities

We have one more innovation map to share—PLC Implementation Map Eight—Sustaining PLCs (Figure 7.3). This innovation map guides us in the development of long-term, school-wide sustainability. We focus on two main categories: distributive leadership and institutionalization. The PLC action plans referred to under distributive leadership were mentioned in Chapter 5 and will be expanded on in Chapter 8 to include action plans for the school or district.

Figure 7.3. Innovation Map Eight—Sustaining Professional Learning Communities

Guiding questions for increasing implementation levels:
- What are our leadership roles and responsibilities in sustaining PLCs?
- How do we commit ourselves, our actions, and our resources to sustain PLCs?
- How do we use policies, practices, or infrastructures to sustain PLCs?

Sustaining PLCs

Sustainability	Level 1 Implementation		Level 2 Implementation		Level 3 Implementation	
Categories	Teacher	Leader	Teacher	Leader	Teacher	Leader
Distributed Leadership Develop and distribute leadership and responsibility for effective execution of PLC plans.	Develops leadership skills and assumes responsibility for development and execution of building or district level PLC action plans.	Identifies leaders and leadership teams, models and develops leadership skills, facilitates development of building or district-level PLC action plans.	Applies leadership skills to the development and execution of building or district-level PLC action plans.	Supports and assesses leadership development and execution of building or district-level PLC action plans.	Assesses leadership skills of self and leadership team to improve execution of building or district-level PLC action plans.	Supports individual and team assessment and coaches for improvements in leadership and execution of building or district-level PLC action plans.
Institutionalizing Identify, develop, monitor, and improve policies, practices, and infrastructures to sustain PLCs.	Identifies and documents existing PLC policies, practices, and infrastructures.	Facilitates identification and documentation of existing PLC policies, practices, and infrastructures.	Identifies threats to sustaining PLCs. Develops policies, practices, and infrastructures to sustain PLCs.	Facilitates planning, adoption, and funding of policies, practices, and infrastructures to sustain PLCs.	Analyzes new district or school concerns or initiatives to align PLC policies, practices, and infrastructures.	Monitors new concerns and initiatives to develop new or realign existing PLC policies, practices, and infrastructures.

As we continue to reflect on the sustainability of PLCs, we can ask what the evidence would "look like" that demonstrates sustainability for improved academic and relational practices in PLCs. The tools and techniques shared in this chapter are examples of what we have used to collect, analyze, and evaluate continuous improvement and sustainability of PLCs. What evidence would be needed for you and your school to ensure that if you left your position tomorrow PLCs would not only continue to exist but would continue to strive for implementation of higher levels of innovation? How can you and your staff assure that the hard work of change continues to make a difference for students and teachers who join you a month, year, or decade from now?

Post Vignette

Based on input and help from her principal PLC and her leadership team, Teresa was able to submit a glowing report to the superintendent. The report shared not only hard data collected from mid-year and end-of-year tests that demonstrated improved student learning but also examples of specific changes to instruction and assessment that demonstrated teacher growth. For instance, examples included the implementation of research-based differentiated instruction coupled with the collective assessment of student work by teachers. After reviewing the report, the superintendent, as well as the school board, expressed a genuine appreciation and respect for the work accomplished. They also articulated a renewed commitment to PLCs. One board member even initiated a conversation about the need to review and update school policies so the board could better support the needed changes identified by the PLC groups.

On a separate note, the superintendent approached Teresa and asked her if she would be interested in moving to the district office to help with curriculum and professional development to increase the effect of PLCs throughout the district. The superintendent had not observed nearly as much growth and commitment to PLCs in other buildings. After reviewing Teresa's report, the superintendent had a stronger understanding of the importance of effective PLC implementation and more importantly, the depth of commitment and energy needed by school leadership to ensure that PLCs became a part of the district's culture.

Teresa contemplated the offer. The opportunity to work more closely with institutionalizing PLCs at the district level was an exciting prospect. Her experiences over the past year only served to strengthen her belief and commitment to use PLCs as a powerful means for changing and honoring the professional work of educators. However, was one year of intentional implementation, with extra care given to the academic and relational components of PLCs, enough to sustain the progress made in her building?

Had her staff worked enough with the innovation maps, the change cycle, and the other processes put in place to continue their efforts?

Teresa reflected on the increased level of energy and commitment expressed by her faculty during their year-end PLC celebration; she noted her leadership team's increased level of confidence and decision making; and she considered the amount of teacher and student growth that had occurred. As a leader, Teresa had effectively led the implementation of PLCs. She had also effectively led the process for sustaining continuous improvement through PLCs. She was where she belonged and would decline the offer to move to the district office. She would offer, instead, to lead through example in her current position. There was still important work to be completed in her building, and she wanted to lead that work.

Just as she had witnessed improved teaching and learning from teacher collaboration, she knew she and her fellow administrators could collectively learn to improve teaching and learning within each of their respective build- ings through collaboration in leadership PLCs. What better way to under- stand and reflect on the challenges and opportunities of PLCs than to personally experience them? Teresa reached for the phone. She would share her idea with her principal PLC, and together they would submit a proposal to the superintendent.

Vignette Analysis

The success of the report submitted by Teresa and her leadership team was not a fluke; it was the outcome of intentional planning and work. Their year of implementation had not been an easy one. It had held a number of challenges as they worked to ensure teacher support for relevant instruction and high accountable for improved student learning. Open communications, support for risk-takers, availability of resources, and procedural changes were developed and maintained in connection with a shared set of expecta- tions for the entire faculty.

It had not been easy work for Teresa. Her own learning had been stretched as she developed plans and procedures that adhered to the purpose and goals that her leadership team formulated. Specifically, Teresa learned a lot about questioning techniques that encouraged reflective thinking, about the importance of teaching and monitoring interpersonal skills in PLCs, and the importance of shared understanding about student learning, adult learning, professional practice, and the needed changes in education. If Teresa had not taken the time to build buy-in for the purpose of PLCs, to build a shared understanding about teaching and learning, and to teach interpersonal and group-process skills, PLC progress would have been minimal. Their use of the innovation maps, the change cycle, and other strategies and resources (i.e., cooperative learning concepts, cognitive coaching techniques, national standards) helped them assess progress through evidence to answered questions, adjust and reflect on their teaching, and demonstrate the effectiveness of their PLCs.

Teresa provided effective leadership in the implementation of PLCs. She also demonstrated appreciation for her faculty's collective knowledge and skill about teaching and learning. She created a culture that honored the uniqueness of students and staff. We believe, as Teresa does, that her faculty will continue to grow and sustain PLCs. We also believe, as Teresa does, that there is merit in expanding PLCs beyond the building level to the district level, especially around the concept of leader PLCs. School leaders need to be held to the same level of accountability for collective professional growth to increase student learning as their teachers.

Reflecting Forward

- How will you institutionalize the use of innovation maps, the change cycle, levels of use protocol, and other resources to support the continuous improvement and the sustainability of PLCs?
- What evidence do you have that documents your school's current level of support for the continuous improvement and sustainability of PLCs?
- What evidence would you need to demonstrate increased support for the continuous improvement and sustainability for PLCs?
- What new learning and resources would you need to increase the support for continuous improvement and sustainability for PLCs?
- What practices and policies would you need to implement to increase the support for the continuous improvement and sustainability for PLCs?
- What evidence would you collect and reflect on to assess progress made with the continuous improvement and sustainability of PLCs?
- Who will you involve when reflecting on your new learning?

With whom will you collaborate to improve the learning or implement the new learning across your school and/or district?

8

Conviction, Courage, and Effort

Vignette 8

Teresa and her principal PLC colleagues were excited. The superintendent was receptive of their plan to strengthen the PLC initiative through the implementation of PLCs for building level principals and central office personnel. They would begin with a summer retreat. Here was their opportunity to share what they had learned, developed, and experienced with one another as they led their building PLC initiative. Equally as exciting was the transformation they were seeing in the superintendent's understanding about her role in the institutionalization of PLCs. When Teresa declined the offer to oversee the implementation of PLCs district-wide, the superintendent began to rethink her approach. The superintendent realized district leadership needed to model what was being expected of building principals and teachers. The district would establish and support leadership PLCs to increase the interdependence between central office and building leaders for shared accountability. With assistance from Teresa and her principal PLC, the superintendent envisioned that the leadership PLCs would result in more effective, sustainable PLCs across the district.

Guiding Questions

- How can we develop an effective leadership action plan?
- What will be the results of our conviction, courage, and efforts?

How Can We Develop an Effective Leadership Action Plan?

We shared in Chapter 1 why we have such a strong passion and commitment to PLCs. We hope after reading our book that others share a similar level of passion and commitment. It is our leadership that will guide our schools and districts in the implementation and sustainability of PLCs. Every proponent of PLCs believes that with full commitment, success is assured. But without an action plan in place to guide implementation of the elements in the innovation maps and the change cycle, commitment remains an abstract wonderful concept, not a reality. The action plan will define for everyone what that commitment means. Thus, in this last chapter we explain the process that might be used to develop a leadership action plan.

A leadership action plan is our roadmap. If grounded in common beliefs and purposes, it helps us avoid problems and take action with confidence and courage. The more confident we are, the more likely we are to have a successful outcome. The action plan supports our self-efficacy and collective efficacy, both essential to change.

Just as our teachers are at various levels of comfort with implementing and sustaining PLCs, so, too, are we as school leaders. With that in mind, we offer an overview of how to move from strong beliefs and buy-in about the value of PLCs to the execution of effective PLCs. Without a specific strategy and process for action, we may find ourselves in an endless quagmire of either planning with no action or action with no planning. Bossidy and Charan (2002) state,

> Everybody talks about change. In recent years, a small industry of changemeisters has preached revolution, reinvention, quantum change, breakthrough thinking, audacious goals, learning organizations, and the like. We're not necessarily debunking this stuff. But unless you translate big thoughts into concrete steps for action, they're pointless. Without execution, the breakthrough thinking breaks down, learning adds no value, people don't meet their stretch goals, and the revolution stops dead in its tracks. What you get is change for the worse, because failure drains the energy from your organization. Repeated failure destroys it. (p. 19)

In a nutshell we need to "plan the work, and work the plan."

Development of a Leadership Action Plan

Marzano, Waters, and McNulty (2005) emphasize the value of "a plan of action that will help any school leader articulate and realize a powerful vision for enhanced achievement of students" (p. 98). Bossidy and Charan (2002) contend, "Execution has to be part of an organization's culture, driving the behavior of all leaders at all levels" (p. 31). We agree and propose that the leadership action plan mirror a process familiar to many in education: identify the purpose; develop specific, measurable, accountable, realistic, and timely (SMART) goals; create action plans that identify the objectives, the activities, the individuals responsible, the timeline, and the expected results; and assess the alignment and effectiveness of the actions through collaboration with others. This same process mirrors the change cycle we have used throughout the book.

Identify the Purpose

Taking time to understand and commit to the purpose of our leadership action plan is just as vital as taking time to develop understanding and commitment to the purpose of PLCs for our teachers. We don't just put a plan together and then go back and see whether it can be of help to us. The purpose can be made clearer by deciding at the beginning: "What do we want to get done? What are the critical issues we need to understand better? And, Why at the end is it going to be helpful to us?" (Bossidy & Charan, 2002, p. 188). We can better define and commit to our purpose by involving our leadership team and our staff in reflecting on "where we are" and "where do we want to be" (Figure 8.1). It may be helpful to use the innovation maps and reflection questions at the end of the chapters to facilitate this ongoing process.

Figure 8.1. Where We Are and Where Do We Want To Be?

Where are we, and what evidence do we have of our current level of implementation?	Where do we want to be, and what evidence do we need to move to the next level of implementation?

Develop SMART Goals

Once the purpose of the leadership action plan is determined, we must set goals for how the work will be accomplished. SMART goals assure that actions are specific, measurable, accountable, realistic, and timely (Figure 8.2). As goals are developed, ask "How can we prioritize our actions based on evidence?" and "How can we distribute accountability among teacher leaders for each of the SMART goals?"

Figure 8.2. SMART Goal Process

SMART: Specific, measurable, accountable, realistic, and timely.

SMART Goal: _____

	Student Learning and Growth	Professional Learning and Growth	PLC Cultural Components	PLC Structural Components
Specific				
Measurable				
Accountable				
Realistic				
Timely				

Develop Individual Action Plans to Meet SMART Goals

Just as we expect teachers to have individual and group accountability within PLCs, school leaders need individual and group accountability for the leadership action plan (Figure 8.3). For school leaders to increase their individual and group accountability, we suggest the development of individual action plans for each SMART goal, distributed accountability for monitoring the plan, and shared accountability for assessing progress on each of the plans. To maintain consistency in the action planning process, we suggest that the PLC action plan form (see Figure 5.14) used in Chapter 5 be used to develop a specific leadership action plan.

Figure 8.3. Professional Learning Communities Action Plan

PLC or Leadership Committee Members: _____

Mission: _____

Vision: _____

Goal(s): _____

Objectives	Activities	People Responsible	Timeline	Completion Date/Results

Once action plans are mapped out, the real work begins. According to Brossidy and Charan, "Execution is a systematic process of rigorously discussing hows and whats, questioning, tenaciously following through, and ensuring accountability" (2002, p. 22). One way to heighten the discussion about the effectiveness of the execution is to ask reflective questions. Based on the work of Bossidy and Charan we developed a set of questions to guide discussions about the cohesiveness and effectiveness of action plans (Figure 8.4).

Figure 8.4. Questions about Cohesiveness and Effectiveness of Action Plans

- What is our assessment of the teaching and learning environment?
- How well do we understand the learning needs of students, teachers, and leaders?
- What other critical issues face the organization?
- What is the best way to increase teacher and/or leader proficiency? What are the obstacles to growth?
- Who or what is competing with the implementation of this essential initiative?
- Can we execute the strategies at the PLC, school, and district levels?
- Are goals and activities balanced for the short and long term?
- What are the important milestones for executing the plan? How will we measure and celebrate them?
- How will the school and/or district align resources to sustain identified changes?

We believe it is important to include teacher leaders in the accountability for PLC implementation. If work is distributed among the teacher leaders, active sharing about successes or concerns in implementation leads to improved execution. Bossidy and Charan (2002) comment, "People practicing [continuous improvement] look for deviations from desired tolerances. When they find them, they move quickly to correct the problem. They use the processes to constantly raise the bar, improving quality and throughput. They use them collaboratively across units to improve how processes work across the organization. It's a relentless pursuit of reality, coupled with processes for constant improvement" (p. 30).

Assess Alignment and Effectiveness of Action Plans

The PLC action plans focus our alignment of resources and efforts at the building level. It may help to view these plans as a system of student and teacher interventions informed by data. Figure 8.5 represents our mental model of such a system.

Figure 8.5. Student and Teacher Intervention System

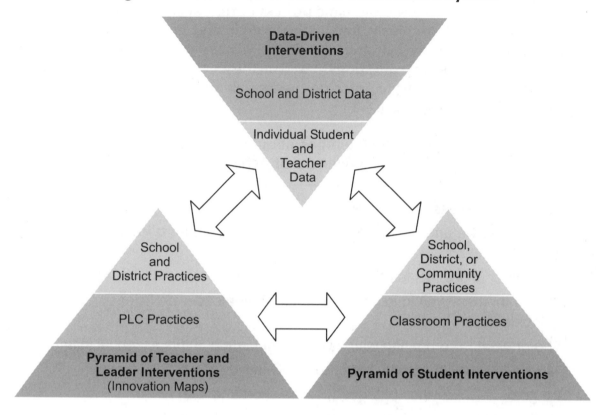

Many schools have identified a pyramid of student interventions (DuFour & Eaker, 1998) to address the needs of students when classroom interventions fail. We believe that this practice is important in the short term to assure that students learn. However, implementing a succession of interventions will not improve the initial teaching experience without feedback to inform and change classroom practices. In the long term, we can only reduce the need for interventions by assuring that classroom interventions are initially successful. This requires the pyramid of interventions for teachers and leaders outlined in the PLC Implementation Innovation Maps. These interventions increase the capacity of teachers, leaders, and schools to address student needs in the classroom and thereby limit the time and resources that must be expended on other interventions to assure student success. Both the teacher and leader pyramid of interventions and the student pyramid of interventions are informed by data. The inverted pyramid of data interventions represents the use of data to drill down to ever increasing levels of specificity to identify individual student and teacher learning needs. All three pyramids function most effectively when there is a conscious effort to share information which is represented by the two-way arrows among the pyramids.

We also need to be aware of the wider context of change initiatives that may play havoc with our plans. When a sudden concern arises at the district, state, national or international level, it is often accompanied with a directive to devote time and attention to the new concern. Witness what happens in a district when the newspapers say that United States students aren't achieving as well as students in foreign countries. Or watch what happens when racial tensions erupt in the community. If we take time to analyze how the issue aligns with our overall leadership action plan, we can avoid knee-jerk reactions and deviation from progress. In our experience, despair and burnout set in when no seeming connection is drawn between existing practices and policies and newly identified concerns. In Chapter 7 we suggested that sustainability is enhanced through analysis of policies, practices, and infrastructures to support PLCs. How can we sustain our action plans in light of outside concerns or new standards that may arise? When a new concern arises, we need to filter that concern through a series of lenses to provide time for reflection and inquiry about the alignment to existing plans. What aspects of our overall teaching and learning system are affected? What best practices currently exist to address this concern in our practices? How are these practices responding to the concern? What future actions might be needed? Many schools and districts use the National Staff Development Council (NSDC) Standards as a framework to assess action plans for cohesiveness among essential elements for effective teaching and learning. We used the standards to complete a document (Figure 8.6) that reflects the action plans, policies, and practices of a sample school. We invite you to look over the document first and then we will walk you through the use of this document as a lens for processing concerns that may arise.

Figure 8.6. Assessing Cohesiveness of Action Plans with the NSDC Standards Framework

NSDC Standards	Best Practice Design	Effects and Future Efforts
Learning Communities Staff development that improves the learning of all students and organizes adults into learning communities whose goals are aligned with those of the school and the district.	• PLCs aligned to goals of district in standards implementation and improvement of instruction. • Regular PLCs encourage reflection with partners and teams of teachers in an ongoing fashion. • Year-long PLCs organized to increase professional practices.	• Teachers value sharing and are committed to sharing with their own grade levels and buildings. • Teachers are requesting more PLC opportunities to allow fellow colleagues to participate. • Teachers are building their own learning communities without guidance. • We are proposing an identified group of PLCs to look at student work to raise achievement on our districts systems targets.
Leadership Staff development that improves the learning of all students; requires skillful school and district leaders who guide continuous instructional improvement.	• Teachers in PLCs become leaders in their buildings through sharing their practice and expectations. • Use district and out-of-district leaders to increase capacity. • PLCs are asked to learn to lead themselves in a selected action research component.	• The PLCs have encouraged and surfaced additional school leaders. • New leaders bring additional instructional skills and effective adult learning models back to their buildings. • The change cycle model of learn, plan, do, reflect, and share is highly valued as the best way to learn and promotes continuous improvement. New communities will use the same format to look at student work.
Resources Staff development that improves the learning of all students; requires resources to support adult learning and collaboration.	• Pay staff to plan, reflect, and coach each other and to share with others as leaders. • Search for partnerships with community and other staff to expand resources. • Use videos on teacher leadership and facilitators to model adult learning and collaboration.	• Learners are looking for additional grant opportunities to continue this work. • Expanded use of available resources in the professional development library, other staff in their buildings or professional development funds, and other grants. • Teachers are valued as resources.

Figure 8.6. Assessing Cohesiveness of Action Plans with the NSDC Standards Framework (continued)

NSDC Standards	Best Practice Design	Effects and Future Efforts
Data-Driven Staff development that improves the learning of all students; uses disaggregated student data to determine adult learning priorities, monitor progress, and help sustain continuous improvements.	• Student innovation map used to measure student understanding and performance on standards-based curriculum. Case studies and student work is examined. • Professional growth innovation map used to measure professional growth using Danielson's framework. • Increased sharing and reflection by teachers to demonstrate application and effect on student learning and teacher practices.	• Marked increase in student achievement observed through innovation map analysis and staff reflections. • Increase in professional growth demonstrated using the Danielson framework with all teachers. • Public sharing of work increases the desire for continuous improvement. • The next area of focus will be on using tuning protocols to examine student work.
Evaluation Staff development that improves the learning of all students; uses multiple sources of information to guide improvements and demonstrate its impact.	• Use of achievement measures on innovation map to assess student impact. • Use of innovation maps, observations, and student work to inform practice. • Use of teacher reflections and Danielson framework to inform professional development needs.	• Student achievement identified through the student innovation map was easy to implement and informed practice. • Participants were able to share their work and demonstrate its impact using multiple methods of presentation. • Participants used examples of student work to share their learning. • The next area of focus will be on using student work and large aggregate test data.
Research-based Staff development that improves the learning of all students; prepares educators to apply research to decisions making.	• PLC learning is based on current research application for successful implementation of standards with focuses on brain-based research, active learning, authentic learning, differentiating learning, and service learning. • The learning communities are based on current research on professional development and adult learning needs.	• PLCs focused practice on effective pedagogical practices related to brain research, authentic learning, differentiation, special needs students, and community. • Adult learning theories are informing PLC structures. • The next area of focus will be on the research behind using student work to inform practice.
Design Staff development that improves the learning of all students; uses learning strategies appropriate to the intended goal.	• The PLCs are designed to improve instructional strategies known to increase the effective implementation of standards. • Research also indicated that shared reflection on student work and other adult learning strategies improve teacher practices and student achievement.	• The goal of using standards-based curriculum guides to assess student growth was achieved. • Staff appreciation and use of reflection on student work and teaching practices increased. • Sharing of student work with others enhances future use and transference to other teaching and learning experiences.

Figure 8.6. Assessing Cohesiveness of Action Plans with the NSDC Standards Framework (continued)

NSDC Standards	Best Practice Design	Effects and Future Efforts
Learning Staff development that improves the learning of all students; applies knowledge about human learning and change.	• A systems model that requires learn, plan, do, and reflect is employed. • Adult learning practices such as active learning, reflection, experiential application, and constructing meaning in context is employed to enhance adult learning.	• Participants expressed appreciation for the change cycle and the power of reflection in their learning. • Reflections indicated that brain-based, constructivist, and relevant approaches were appreciated. • The sense of professional community with others was appreciated and desired. • More time was identified for PLCs based on evidence of effectiveness.
Collaboration Staff development that improves the learning of all students; provides educators with the knowledge and skills to collaborate.	• Each PLC is designed to require collaboration, discussion, and reflection with other teachers • Each PLC has an additional expectation to share beyond the PLC with other teachers. • The learning community measures collaboration skills and actively teaches reflection techniques.	• The appreciation of sharing will make ongoing collaboration more likely. • Reflections indicate a commitment to share with others at the team, building, district, and cross-district level. • Teachers value collaboration with other districts and desire more. • The next area of focus will be on reflective practice and collaboration protocols to examine student work.
Equity Staff development that improves the learning of all students; prepares educators to understand and appreciate all students, create safe, orderly, and supportive learning environments, and hold high expectations for students' academic achievement.	• PLCs are designed to honor the diverse learning needs of students and teachers. • PLCs model the need for active, authentic, applied, and reflective work to support learning. • PLCs use innovation maps to define expectations for students and teachers.	• Expansion of this opportunity to all staff and different schools provided a wider perspective of student needs. • Strategies expanded expectations for student achievement, and professional growth was encouraged by increased student achievement. • When teachers experienced safe, supportive environments themselves, they created like environments for students.

Figure 8.6. Assessing Cohesiveness of Action Plans with the NSDC Standards Framework (continued)

NSDC Standards	Best Practice Design	Effects and Future Efforts
Quality Teaching Staff development that improves the learning of all students, deepens educators' content knowledge, provides them with research-based instructional strategies to assist students in meeting rigorous academic standards, and prepares them to use various types of classroom assessments appropriately.	• Each PLC is designed to expand the content application of teachers and students based on research on instructional strategies on active, authentic, accommodated, differentiated, and service learning. • Multiple forms of assessment are modeled and practiced in each PLC. • The learning community continuously reflects on assessing quality teaching by other teachers and themselves.	• Teachers shared strategies and helped others at their schools use them. • Teachers became accustomed to alternative ways of assessing student and teacher work. • Teachers expressed the desire to expand their use of strategies and assessments with other teachers. • The next area of focus will be to help teachers define higher quality teaching and feedback based on student work protocols.
Family involvement Staff development that improves the learning of all students; provides educators with knowledge and skills to involve families and other stakeholders.	• Facilitators well versed in each instructional strategy are tapped to enhance educators' knowledge and skills. • Direct involvement of community members in service learning helps to build a sense of community and identify genuine needs. • Community needs, issues, problems, or applications are addressed throughout each PLC.	• Service learning and applied learning participants pursued expansion of community stakeholders, assistance, and audiences. • Increased student excitement about learning led to increased parent interest. • A roundtable discussion is planned to help teachers and community members share their needs and assets.

Let's follow a concern using Figure 8.6. Suddenly, issues of racial conflict erupt in the community, and the district directs each school to provide training on diversity, demonstrating the district's commitment to addressing the concern. This can be viewed through the "equity" lens in the first column of the document. In the second column, we can see that our PLCs are honoring diverse learning needs through authentic, active, applied work and that we are using innovation maps to define clear expectations for students and teachers. In column three, this results in an expansion of perspectives about student needs, improved strategies for student achievement, and development of safe and supportive learning environments. Therefore, if any additional learning is needed to address the concern, it can be addressed through increasing awareness of needs, new strategies to address those needs, and refinements to safe and supporting learning environments. A new initiative is not needed, and our action plan is not derailed.

This level of cohesion in analyzing and monitoring challenges against existing policies, practices, and infrastructures indicates a high level of institutionalization of PLCs. Leaders can use Figure 7.3. (PLC Implementation Innovation Map Eight—Sustaining PLCs) to assess and increase distributed leadership responsibility for PLC action plans and for institutionalization of changes.

What Will Be the Results of Our Conviction, Courage, and Efforts?

Improved collaboration between teachers and leaders through effective PLCs leads to four important results: improved student achievement regardless of demographics, increased teacher proficiency in using research-based practices, increased student sense of belonging and efficacy, and increased sense of belonging and efficacy for teachers and leaders. The road to collaboration is much more complex than most believe. As we have seen, it takes much more than putting teachers together physically to produce collaborative work. When the road gets rough, our action plans clarify our convictions and give us the courage to stay the course.

One principal faced his teaching staff at the beginning of the year stating that he had never been more afraid of the direction he was requesting his staff to take. He explained that the PLC initiative would be either wildly successful or a total bust but he believed in his staff enough to take a leap of faith. They developed common convictions, faced challenges with courage, applied amazing effort and at the conclusion of the year they had, through their PLCs, implemented several effective teaching practices that resulted in significant student gains on the state tests. The day the results were announced, the principal called his staff together to celebrate their willingness to commit to an unknown adventure that resulted in student success. Then, he asked, "What do you think we can do next year?"

As this school determines what they can do next year, they can use the change analysis framework (Figure 8.7) we shared in Chapter 1 (see Figure 1.2) to guide them through reflection and documentation that honors and celebrates their past work but also supports construction of their desired future to assure continued change. The following questions will guide such a reflective celebration and planning process.

- What is our history from this past year (student learning, professional learning, PLC learning)?
- What are our beliefs and values now?
- What assumptions do we have about how students learn, how adults learn, how adults interact, how we align our goals, curriculum, instruction, assessment, and resources?
- What are the policies and practices that we developed to increase learning for students and adults this last year?
- What is our desired state for next year regarding history, beliefs and values, assumptions, and policies and practices?
- What are the structural and cultural assets and barriers? How can we remove barriers and enhance or create assets?
- How can we use the innovation maps, SMART goals, and action plans to move us to our desired state by the end of next year?

Figure 8.7. Change Analysis Framework

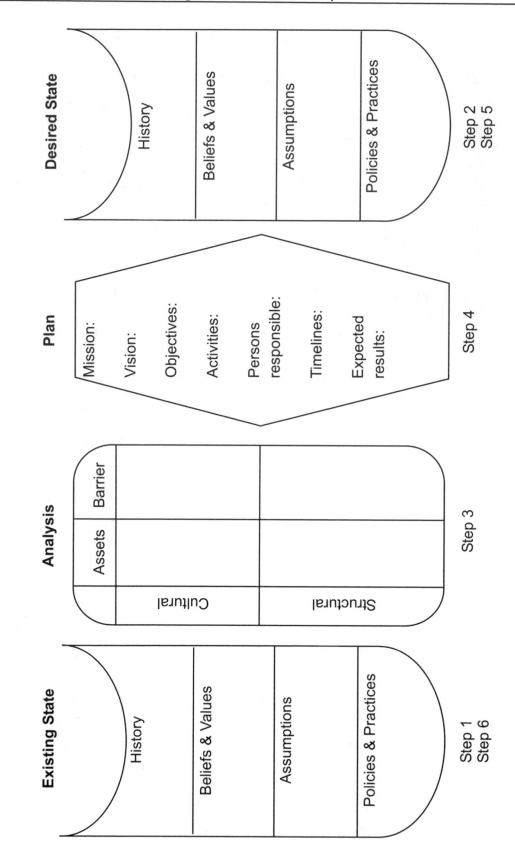

When we model and support the risk taking needed and celebrate the successes gained from our commitment to action plans, we will witness the remarkable results we believe are possible through PLCs. If we, as school leaders, do not face the challenges of implementing and sustaining PLCs with conviction, courage, and effort, who will? If not me, who?

Post Vignette

The leadership retreat had been received well, but there were growing pains in the leadership PLCs throughout the year, just as there had been for Teresa's teacher PLCs. Reflecting back over the course of events and experiences, Teresa realized that it had been one of the more rewarding years of her career—not that it was without struggles and challenges, but it was also filled with hope and renewed passion. Increased commitment to continued change came from evidence of sustainable growth in her building PLCs as well as evidence of growth and sustainability across the district.

Teresa really felt she was becoming a more effective leader. The action plans she had developed served as an essential guide to align changes and adjustments in her building to support student and teacher growth. The more time she spent in her leadership PLC the more she valued the learning and the relationships they were building. She was amazed at how much the involvement of the superintendent and other central office personnel in PLCs increased communication and understanding between schools and district office.

Unlike last year, where they had two days to craft the state of the district message, they had been gathering and analyzing evidence throughout the year and had been working on the report all year long. The state of the district message celebrated impressive successes in student learning and teacher growth from changes made through PLCs.

As an administrative team, they now had more relevant evidence for decision-making. The systemic implementation of action plans allowed the superintendent and principals to determine where additional resources were needed. Leaders were better able to investigate specific concerns that arose in the community and how they could address them with their plans. Leaders could collaborate on changes yet needed and refocus on improvements for the next year. Leaders spoke with greater confidence about their ability to meet future challenges through shared responsibility. More than ever, Teresa understood the collective impact of PLCs. She had ample evidence demonstrating that teachers and school leaders were guaranteeing the success of each student. This success increased her conviction and courage to lead.

Vignette Analysis

In our book, Teresa and the district have turned an important corner in developing collective responsibility for the development of effective PLCs. Only through working in a PLC can school leaders understand how to lead PLCs. Shared action plans across the district led to increased alignment of district goals, relationships, resources, and actions. There is greater collaboration and confidence, demonstrating an increase in trust among leaders. Their commitment to plan, execute, and share results produced effective documentation and cause for celebration. They have discovered the importance of aligned behavior and action plans in producing teacher growth and student results.

Reflecting Forward

- What would you need to develop your leadership action plan?
- What would you need to implement your leadership action plan?
- What evidence would you collect and reflect on to assess the execution of your action plans?
- Who will you involve when reflecting on the execution of your action plans?
- With whom will you collaborate to align your action plans across your school and /or district?
- How will you align actions and resources in a systematic approach to institutionalize PLCs as a means to address future concerns?

References

Selected References to Deepen Understanding of Adult Learning, Change Processes, and Professional Learning Communities

This appendix is provided for readers who wish to extend their understanding of adult learning theories and practices, theories about the change process, and research on professional learning communities. Complete citations for authors are listed in the reference section.

Adult Learning

Adult learning theorists: Brookfield (1986), Knowles et al. (1984), Knowles, et al. (1998), Kolb (1984), Merriam & Cafferella (1999), and Mezirow (2000).

Constructivist theorists: Brooks & Brooks (1993), Fosnot (1996), and Lambert (1995).

Five key adult learning needs for creating effective adult learning environments.

1. Adult learners need to learn through experience within a real setting or context (Brookfield, 1986; Caine & Caine, 1997a, 1997b; Knowles et al., 1998; Kolb, 1984; Merriam & Cafferella, 1999; Mezirow, 2000; Wheatley, 1992).

2. Learning for adults is socially transacted, negotiated, relationship-based, and collaborative (Belinky & Stanton, 2000; Brookfield, 1986, 1995; Caine & Caine, 1997a, 1997b; Daloz, 2000; Evans, 1996; Fullan, 1993, 2002; Lambert, 1995a, 1995b; Lieberman et al., 1988; Mezirow, 2000; Senge, 1995; Stigler & Hiebert; 1999; Taylor, 2000; Vygotsky, 1978).

3. A key difference between adult learning and pedagogy seems to be that adults prefer self-directed learning (Brookfield, 1986; Cross, 1981; Knowles et al., 1998; Kolb, 1984; Merriam & Cafferella, 1999; Mezirow, 2000; Vella, 1994; Wheatley, 1992).

4. There seems to be wide agreement that adults need to participate in individual or group reflection on their learning (Annenberg Foundation, 2002; Belinky & Stanton, 2000; Brookfield, 1986; Caine & Caine, 1997a, 1997b; Costa & Garmston; 2002; Fivush, 2000; Foord, 2004; Glickman, 2002; Lambert, 1995a; Merriam & Cafferella, 1999; Mezirow, 1998, 2000; Schon, 1987a, 1987b; Senge, et al., 2000; Wheatley, 1992; York-Barr et al., 2001).

5. There is also an increasing awareness of the need to learn in a community of learners (Collay et al., 1998; Daloz, 2000; DuFour & Eaker, 1998; Hord, 2004; Louis & Kruse, 1995; Sergiovanni, 1994).

Change Processes

- Changing goals, roles, rules, structures, or measurements (Evans, 1996; Fullan, 1995; Hall & Hord, 2001).
- School cultural change (Bolman & Deal, 1997; Evans, 1996; Senge, et al., 2000; Sergiovanni, 1996).
- School change agents (Evans, 1996; Hammerman, 1999; Hargreaves, 1994; Stigler & Hiebert, 1999).
- Change process (Foord, 2004; Fullan, 1993, 1995; Guskey, 2000; Hall & Hord, 2001; McCarthy & Leflar, 1983; Stigler & Hiebert, 1999; Toole, 2001).
- Teacher change and collegiality (Barth, 1990; Caine & Caine, 1997b; Hargreaves, 1994; Lieberman et al., 1988).

Professional Learning Communities

- Learning communities (Bransford et al., 2000; Collay et al., 1998; DuFour & Eaker, 1998; DuFour et al., 2004; DuFour et al., 2005; DuFour et al., 2006; Louis et al., 1995; McLaughlin 1993; McLaughlin & Talbert, 2006; Sergiovanni, 1994; Toole, 2001).
- Collective efficacy and collegiality (Goddard et al., 2004; Little, 1990; Hargreaves, 1994; Talbert & McLaughlin, 2002).
- Professional learning community leadership (Hord, 2004).
- Cooperative and collaborative learning (Barkley et al., 2006; Johnson et al., 2006).

References

Annenberg Foundation & Chicago Learning Collaborative. (2002). Looking at student work. Providence, RI: Brown University. Retrieved June 11, 2008, from http://www.lasw.org/methods/html.

Barkley, E. F., Cross, K. P., & Major, C. H. (2005). *Collaborative learning techniques.* San Francisco: Jossey-Bass.

Barth, R. (1990). *Improving schools from within: Teachers, parents, and principals can make the difference.* San Francisco: Jossey-Bass.

Barth, R. (2001). *Learning by heart.* San Francisco: Jossey-Bass.

Belinky, M. F., & Stanton, A. V. (2000). Inequalities, development and connected knowing. In J. Mezirow et al. (Eds.), *Learning as transformation* (pp. 71–103). San Francisco: Jossey-Bass.

Bernhardt, V. (2005). *Using data to improve student learning.* Larchmont, NY: Eye on Education.

Blankstein, A.M. (2004). *Failure is not an option: Six principles that guide student achievement in high-performing schools.* San Francisco: Corwin.

Bolman, L. G., & Deal, T. E. (1997). *Reframing organizations.* San Francisco: Jossey-Bass.

Bossidy, L., & Charan, R. (2002). *Execution: The discipline of getting things done.* New York: Crown Business.

Bransford, J. D., Brown, A. L., & Cocking, R. R. (Eds.). (2000). *How people learn.* Washington, DC: National Academy Press.

Brookfield, S. D. (1986). *Understanding and facilitating adult learning.* San Francisco: Jossey-Bass.

Brookfield, S. D. (1995). *Becoming a critically reflective teacher.* San Francisco: Jossey-Bass.

Brooks, J. G., & Brooks, M. G. (1993). *In search of understanding: The case for constructivist classrooms.* Alexandria, VA: Association for Supervision and Curriculum Development.

Butler, K. (1987). *Learning and teaching style: In theory and practice.* Columbia, CT: The Learner's Dimension.

Caine, R. N., & Caine, G. (1997a). *Unleashing the power of perceptual change.* Alexandria, VA: Association for Supervision and Curriculum Development.

Caine, R. N., & Caine, G. (1997b). *Education on the edge of possibility.* Alexandria, VA: Association for Supervision and Curriculum Development.

Cialdini, R. B. (2007). *Influence: The psychology of persuasion.* New York: HarperCollins.

Collay, M., Dunlap, D., Enloe, W., & Gagnon, G. W. (1998). *Learning circles.* San Francisco: Corwin Press.

Cooperrider, D. L., & Whitney, D. (2005). *Appreciative inquiry: A positive revolution in change.* San Francisco: Berrett-Koehler.

Costa, A. L., & Garmston, R. J. (2002). *Cognitive coaching* (2nd ed.). Norwood, MA: Christopher-Gordon.

Costa, A. L., & Garmston, R. J. (2005). *Cognitive coaching foundation seminar learning guide.* Highlands Ranch, CO: Center for Cognitive Coaching.

Covey, S. R. (1989). *The 7 habits of highly effective people: Powerful lessons in personal change.* New York: Simon & Schuster.

Cross, K. P. (1981). *Adults as learners.* San Francisco: Jossey-Bass.

Daloz, L.A. (2000). Transformative learning for the common good. In J. Mezirow, et al. (Eds.), *Learning as transformation* (pp. 103–125). San Francisco: Jossey-Bass.

Danielson, C. (1996). *Enhancing professional practice.* Alexandria, VA: Association for Supervision and Curriculum Development.

Danielson, C. (2006). *Teachers leadership that strengthens professional practice.* Alexandria, VA: Association for Supervision and Curriculum Development.

Downey, C. L., Steffy, B. E., English, F. W., & Frase, L. E. (2004). *The three-minute classroom walk-through: Changing school supervisory practice one teacher at a time.* San Francisco: Corwin Press.

DuFour, R., DuFour, R., Eaker, R., & Karhanek, G. (2004). *Whatever it takes.* Bloomington, IN: National Education Service.

DuFour, R., DuFour, R., Eaker, R., & Many, T. (2006). *Learning by doing: A handbook for professional learning communities at work.* Bloomington, IN: Solution Tree.

DuFour, R., & Eaker, R. (1998). *Professional learning communities at work.* Alexandria, VA: Association for Supervision and Curriculum Development.

DuFour, R., Eaker, R., & DuFour, R. (Eds.). (2005). *On common ground: The power of professional communities.* Bloomington, IN: National Educational Service.

Dwyer, C. A. (1994). *Praxis III: Classroom performance assessments assessment criteria.* Princeton, NJ: Educational Testing Service.

E-Lead: Leadership for student success. A partnership of the Laboratory for Student Success and the Institute for Educational Leadership. Retrieved January 2, 2008, from http://www.e.lead.org.

Evans, R. (1996). *The human side of change.* San Francisco: Jossey-Bass.

Fivush, R. (2000). Accuracy, authority, and voice: feminist perspectives on autobiographical memory. In P. H. Miller & E. K. Scholnick (Eds.), *Toward a feminist developmental psychology* (pp. 85–107). New York: Routledge.

Foord, K. A. (2004). *Staff development that influences changes in teacher's beliefs and practices.* Unpublished dissertation. St. Paul, MN: Hamline University

Fosnot, C. (1996). Constructivism: A psychological theory of learning. In C. Fosnot (Ed.), *Constructivism* (pp. 8–33). New York: Teachers College Press.

Fullan, M. (1993). *Change forces.* Bristol, PA: The Falmer Press.

Fullan, M. (1995). Creating quality communities. In Gozdz, K. (Ed.), *Community building: Renewing spirit and learning in business* (pp. 49–55). San Francisco: New Leaders Press.

Fullan, M. (2002, May). The change leader. *Educational Leadership, 59*(8). Alexandria VA: Association for Supervision and Curriculum Development.

Glickman, C. D. (2002). *Leadership for learning.* Alexandria, VA: Association for Supervision and Curriculum Development.

Glickman, C. D., Gordon, S. P., & Ross-Gordon, J. M. (2004). *SuperVision and instructional leadership: A developmental approach.* New York: Pearson.

Goddard, R. D., Hoy, W. K., & Hoy, A. W. (2004, April). Collective efficacy beliefs: Theoretical developments, empirical evidence, and future directions. *Educational Researcher, 33*(3), 3–13.

Goldberg, M. (1998). *The art of the question: A guide to short-term, question-centered therapy.* New York: John Wiley & Sons, Inc.

Goleman, D. (2007). *Social intelligence: The new science of human relationships.* New York: Bantam.

Guskey, T. R. (2000). *Evaluating professional development.* San Francisco: Corwin Press.

Hall, G. E., & Hord, S. M. (2001). *Implementing change: Patterns, principles, and potholes.* Boston: Allyn and Bacon.

Hammerman, J. K. (1999). Teacher inquiry groups: Collaborative explorations of changing practice. In M. Z. Solomon (Ed.), *The diagnostic teacher* (p. xx). New York: Teachers College Press.

Hargreaves, A. (1994). *Changing teachers, changing times.* New York: Teachers College Press.

Hiemstra, R., & Sisco, B. (1990). *Individualized instruction: Making learning personal, empowering, and successful.* San Francisco: Jossey-Bass.

Hord, S. M. (1997). *Professional learning communities: Communities of continuous inquiry and improvement.* Austin, TX: Southwest Educational Development Laboratory. Retrieved October 25, 2003, from http://www.sedl.org/pubs/change34/welcome.html.

Hord, S. (Ed.). (2004). *Learning together, leading together: Changing schools through professional learning communities.* New York: Teachers College Press and Oxford, OH: National Staff Development Council.

Howard, R. (Producer). (2002). *A beautiful mind* [Motion picture]. United States: Universal Studios.

Johnson, D. W., Johnson, R. T. & Holubec, E. J. (1994). *Cooperative learning in the classroom.* Edina, MN: Interaction Book Company.

Johnson, D. W., Johnson, R. T, & Smith, K. A (2006). *Active learning: Cooperation in the college classroom.* Edina, MN: Interaction Book Company.

Joyce, B., & Showers, B. (1988, 2002). *Student achievement through staff development.* Arlington, VA: Association for Supervision and Curriculum Development.

Killion, J. (2002). *Assessing impact.* Oxford, OH: National Staff Development Council.

Kolb, D. A. (1984). *Experiential learning: Experience as the source of learning and development.* Englewood Cliffs, NJ: Prentice Hall.

Knowles, M. S., et al. (1984). *Andragogy in action.* San Francisco: Jossey-Bass.

Knowles, M. S, Holton, E. F., & Swanson, R. A. (1998). *The adult learner* (5th ed). Boston, MA: Butterworth-Heinemann.

Lambert, L. (1995a). Leading the conversations. In L. Lambert, D. Walker, D. P. Zimmerman, et al., *The constructivist leader* (pp. 83–103). New York: Teachers College Press.

Lambert, L. (1995b). Toward a theory of constructivist leadership. In L. Lambert, D. Walker, D. P. Zimmerman, et al., *The constructivist leader* (pp. 28–51). New York: Teachers College Press.

Lee, V. E., & Smith, J. B. (1995). Effects of high school restructuring and size on gains in achievement and engagement for early secondary school students. *Sociology of Education, 68,* 241–270.

Lee, V. E., & Smith, J. B. (1996). Collective responsibility for learning and its effects on gains in achievement for early secondary school students. *American Journal of Education, 104,* 103–147.

Lee, V. E., Smith, J. B., & Croninger, R. G. (1997). How high school organization influences the equitable distribution of learning in mathematics and science. *Sociology of Education, 70,* 128–150.

Leverett, L. (2002). *Warriors to advance equity: An argument for distributing leadership. Spotlight on student success.* Philadelphia, PA: The Laboratory for Student Success, the Mid-Atlantic Regional Educational Laboratory, Temple University Center for Research in Human Development and Education.

Lieberman, A., Saxl, E. R., Miles, M. B. (1988). Teacher leadership: ideology and practice. In A. Lieberman (Ed.), *Building a professional culture in schools* (pp. 148–166). New York: Teachers College Press.

Little, J. W. (1990, Summer). The persistency of privacy: Autonomy and initiative in teachers' professional relations. *Teachers college record, 91* (4), 509–536. New York: Teachers College, Columbia University.

Looking at student work. (2008). Retrieved June 11, 2008, from http://www.lasw.org.

Louis, K. S., & Kruse, S. D. (1995). Developing professional community in new and restructuring urban schools. In K. S. Louis, S. D. Kruse, et al., *Professionalism and community* (pp. 187–207). Thousand Oaks, CA: Corwin Press.

Louis, K. S., Kruse, S. D., & Bryk, A. S. (1995). An emerging framework for analyzing school-based professional community. In K. S. Louis, S. D. Kruse, et al., *Professionalism and community* (pp. 23–44). Thousand Oaks, CA: Corwin Press.

Marzano, B., & Pickering, D. (1997). *Dimensions of learning.*

Marzano, R. J., Pickering, D. J., & Pollack, J. B. (2001). *Classroom instruction that works: Research-based strategies for increasing student achievement.* Alexandria, VA: Association for Supervision and Curriculum Development.

Marzano, R. J., Waters, T., & McNulty, B. (2005). *School leadership that works: From research to results.* Alexandria, VA: Association for Supervision and Curriculum Development and Aurora, CO: Mid-continent Research for Education and Learning.

McCarthy, B. (1987). *The 4MAT system.* Wauconda, IL: EXCEL, Inc.

McCarthy, B., & Leflar, S. (1983). *4MAT in action.* Wauconda, IL: EXCEL, Inc.

McCarthy, B., St. Germain, C., & Lippitt, L. (2002). *The 4MAT research guide.* Wauconda, IL: About Learning, Inc.

McLaughlin, M. W. (1993). What matters most in teachers' workplace context? In J. W. Little & M. W. McLaughlin, *Teachers' work: Individuals, colleagues, and contexts* (pp. 79–103). New York: Teachers College Press.

McLaughlin, M. W., & Talbert, J. E. (2006). *Building school-based teacher learning communities.* New York: Teachers College Press.

McNamee, S., & Gergen, K. J. (1999). *Relational responsibility.* Thousand Oaks, CA: Sage Publications.

Merriam, S. B., & Caffarella, R. S. (1999). *Learning in adulthood* (2nd ed.). San Francisco: Jossey-Bass.

Merriam, S. B., Caffarella, R. S., & Baumgartner, L. M. (2007). *Learning in adulthood: A comprehensive guide.* San Francisco: Wiley.

Mezirow, J., & Associates, (2000). *Learning as transformation: Critical perspectives on a theory in progress,* (pp. 3–34). San Francisco: Jossey-Bass.

Miller, P. H. (2000). The development of interconnected thinking. In Miller, P. H., & Scholnick, E. K. (Eds.) *Toward a feminist developmental psychology* (pp. 45–60). New York: Routledge.

Murphy, C., & Lick, D. (1998). *Whole-faculty study groups: A powerful way to change schools and enhance learning.* Thousand Oaks, CA: Corwin Press, Inc.

National Board for Professional Teaching Standards (NBPTS). (1989). *Toward high and rigorous standards for the teaching profession.* Ann Arbor, MI: Author.

National Commission on Teaching and America's Future (NCTAF). (1997). *Doing what matters: Investing in quality teaching.* New York: Author.

National Staff Development Council. (2001). NSDC's Standards for Staff Development. Retrieved June 11, 2008 from http://www.nsdc.org/standards/index.cfm.

Newman, F. M., Wehlage, G. G., Secada, W. G., et al. (1996). *Authentic achievement: Restructuring schools for intellectual quality.* San Francisco: Jossey-Bass.

Pajak, E. (2003). *Honoring diverse teaching styles: A guide for supervisors.* Alexandria, VA: Association for Supervision and Curriculum Development.

Pfeffer, J., & Sutton, R. I. (2000). *The knowing-doing gap.* Boston: Harvard Business School Press.

Rosenholtz, S. J. (1991). *Teachers' workplace.* New York: Teachers College Press.

Rubin, J. Z., Pruitt, D.G., Kim, S. H. (1994). *Social conflict: Escalation, stalemate, and settlement.* New York: McGraw-Hill.

Schank, R. C. (1990). *Tell me a story: Narrative and intelligence.* Evanston, IL: Northwestern University Press.

Scheffert, D., Anderson, M., & Anderson, S. (1999). *Facilitation resources,* Vols. 1–7. Hubert H. Humphrey Institute of PUblic Affaris and University of Minnesota Extension. University of Minnesota Extension Distribution Center: St. Paul, MN.

Schlechty, P. C. (1997). *Inventing better schools: An action plan for educational reform.* San Francisco: Jossey-Bass.

Schmoker, M. (1996). *Results: The key to continuous school improvement* (2nd ed.). Alexandria, VA: Association for Supervision and Curriculum Development.

Schon, D. A. (1987a). *Educating the reflective practitioner. San Francisco: Jossey-Bass.*

Schon, D. A. (1987b). *Educating the reflective practitioner* (presentation). American Educational Research Association, Washington, DC. Retrieved October 11, 2001, from http://www.educ.queensu.ca/~ar/schon87.htm.

Scott, L. A. & Ingels, S. J. (2007, September). Interpreting 12˙-graders' NAEP-scaled mathematics performance using high school predictors and postsecondary outcomes from the National Education Longitudinal Study of 1988 (NELS:88).Washington, D. C.: Institute of Education Sciences. Retrieved June 11, 2008 from http://nces.ed.gov/surveys/NELS88/.

Senge, P. (1995). Creating quality communities. In K. Gozdz (Ed.), *Community building* (pp. 49–55). San Francisco: New Leaders Press.

Senge, P., Cambron-McCabe, N., Lucas, T., Smith, B., Dutton, J., & Kleiner, A. (2000). *Schools that learn.* New York: Doubleday.

Sergiovanni, T. J. (1994). *Building community in schools.* San Francisco: Jossey-Bass.

Sergiovanni, T. J. (1996). *Leadership for the schoolhouse.* San Francisco: Jossey-Bass.

Singleton, G., & Linton, C. (2006). *Courageous conversations about race.* Thousand Oaks, CA: Corwin Press.

Southeast Center for Teaching Quality. (2004). *Students learn more from National Board Certified teachers.* Retrieved March 19, 20004, from http://www.teachingquality.org/resources/html/NBPTS_Goldhaber.htm.

Sparks, D. (April, 2002). Amplifying positive deviance in schools. *Results*, OH: National Staff Development Council.

Sparks, D. (2005). The final 2%. *Journal of the National Staff Development Council, 26* (2), 8–15.

Stigler, J. W., & Hiebert, J. (1999). *The teaching gap.* New York: The Free Press.

Stiggins, R. J., Arter, J. A., Chappuis, J., & Chappuis, S. (2006). *Classroom assessment for student learning.* Portland, OR: Educational Testing Service.

Strong, J. H. (2002). *Qualities of effective teachers.* Alexandria, VA: Association for Supervision and Curriculum Development.

Talbert, J. E., & McLaughlin, M. W. (2002). Professional communities and the artisan model of teaching. *Teachers and Teaching: Theory and Practice, 8* (3/4), 325–343.

Taylor, E. W. (2000). Analyzing research on transformative learning. In J. Mezirow, et al., *Learning as transformation* (pp. 285–329). San Francisco: Jossey-Bass.

Toole, J. C. (2001, May). *Mental models, professional learning community, and the deep structure of school improvement: Case studies of service-learning.* Unpublished dissertation.

Treffinger, D. J., Isaksen, S. G., & Dorval, K. B. (2000). *Creative problem solving: An introduction.* Waco, TX: Prufrock Press.

Vella, J. (1994). *Learning to listen, learning to teach: The power of dialogue in educating adults.* San Francisco: Jossey-Bass.

Vygotsky, L. S. (1978). *Mind in society: The development of higher psychological processes.* Cambridge MA: Harvard University Press.

Wheatley, M. (1992). *Leadership and the new science.* San Francisco, CA.: Berrett-Koehler.

Wiggins, G. P., & McTighe, J. (2005). *Understanding by design.* Alexandria, VA: Association for Curriculum and Supervision.

Yasumoto, V. M., Uekawa, K., & Bidwell, C. E. (2001). The collegial focus and high school student's achievement. *Sociology of Education, 74,* 181–209.

York-Barr, J., Sommers, W. A., Ghere, G. S., & Montie, J. (2001). *Reflective practice to improve schools.* San Francisco: Corwin Press.

Index